Dinner Tonight

Dinner Tonight

200 Fast + Fresh Mealtime Solutions

Lucy Waverman

Canadian Cataloguing in Publication Data

Waverman, Lucy
Dinner tonight: 200 fast and fresh mealtime solutions

ISBN: 0-679-30957-8

1. Quick and easy cookery. I. Title

TX833.5.W375 1998   641.5'55   C98-931208-9

Cover and interior photography: Vince Noguchi
Food stylist: Jennifer McLagan
Cover and interior design: Sharon Foster Design

Printed and bound in Canada

10 9 8 7 6 5 4 3 2 1

Contents

Acknowledgments

You cannot write a cookbook in isolation. Like all books, this one is the result of the help, advice and enthusiasm of others. I want to thank my agent, Jan Whitford, who persuaded me that writing another cookbook was a worthwhile task, and Doug Pepper, whose excitement about the project brought me to Random House.

With cookbooks it is the testers who really make the difference. Penny Higgins is the best, with her knowledge, her testing skills and her ability to simplify recipes while still getting the same results. Shelley Tanaka once again waved her magic over the manuscript and put it into readable form.

Food stylist Jennifer McLagan has impeccable taste and a great artistic sense. Vince Noguchi's photographic skills make all food look mouth-watering. Sharon Foster succeeded so well in making the book look different while still being accessible. And warmest thanks to Sarah Davies, who pulled the whole thing together.

Four generations of my family have been attracted to the food business. My parents have always enjoyed good food, and my mother is the most creative cook I know, some of her ideas are in this book. My children all cook. My daughter Emma, a great cook and food writer herself, gave her comments and tested recipes. My daughter Katie moved to San Francisco and gave me an excuse to visit her and learn more about West Coast food and restaurants. Alex, my stepson, paid me a great compliment when he went into the restaurant business and finally learned to like fish. My husband, Bruce, is the taster of all recipes, the soother of all tensions and a tough editor. Our shared enjoyment of food and wine makes this book his, too.

Finally, to Marilyn Dennis, and to Chrissie Rejman and Grace Torterelli, who produce my segments on CityLine and are so appreciative of my style; to Cecily Ross and my editors at the *Globe and Mail* for giving me the freedom to focus on what I believe is important in food; and to Nancy Cardinal and the editors at *Food and Drink* for their support for my food writing—a huge thank-you.

Introduction

I love food. Food that satisfies the taste buds and leaves you feeling contented. Food that makes your mouth water just at the thought of it. Think of mounds of crunchy, golden roasted vegetables; a pristine asparagus salad with a touch of shaved Parmesan, glistening with lemon juice and the best olive oil; perfectly roasted juicy chicken with waves of mashed potatoes; Asian noodle soup full of fresh, complex flavors. Tasty, eclectic food without pretensions, as well as being easy and quick to prepare. **Dinner Tonight** is the result of my search for this kind of flavorful and soul-satisfying food.

So many of us are working long hours; we are under constant pressure, with too little time for family and friends. Yet many of us still want dinner to be a special time in a busy day. Classes at cooking schools are overflowing. Young people leading hectic lives are finding that having friends over for a meal is a terrific social opportunity, and that enjoying a simple dinner with family can be a welcome respite from the stresses of daily life. A well-equipped store cupboard, good recipes and a little time management can make these occasions easier to achieve.

As we travel the world and the world comes to us, the foods and techniques of other countries have made their way into our lives. I like to use local, seasonal produce whenever possible, as well as ingredients and techniques from other cultures. A touch of Thai, rustic Italian, some Mediterranean magic and Japanese and Caribbean flavorings are all part of **Dinner Tonight**

I have made every recipe in this book for my family and friends, and many have been shared with viewers of CityLine as well as readers of my *Globe and Mail* column, *Food and Drink*, *Style at Home*, *House and Home* and *Canadian Gardening*. **Dinner Tonight** is full of recipes that I love to cook, and I hope you will, too.

CHAPTER 1

The Store Cupboard

Life itself is the proper binge.
— Julia Child

The Store Cupboard

Tired from work, no food at home, hungry, can't be bothered to shop, and take-out food has no appeal—it's a familiar scenario. But if you have a well-stocked store cupboard, you'll have the luxury of being able to cook a quick dinner without having to shop first.

Your store cupboard should stock basic ingredients and seasonings for everyday cooking. It will serve as a back-up when you can't get to the store.

My store cupboard indicates how we eat at home. Yours will reflect your own style, but here is a basic list.

Seasonings and Condiments

Dijon mustard (*a staple for salad dressings as well as many other dishes*)
dry mustard
ketchup
pesto
hot pepper sauce
Worcestershire sauce
soy sauce
Asian chili sauce (*such as sambal oelek*)
Hoisin sauce
table salt
kosher salt
black peppercorns (*use a pepper mill and always add freshly ground pepper to dishes; ground pepper loses its potency almost immediately*)
good-quality chicken and beef stock cubes (*read the ingredients and make sure chicken or beef appears near the top of the list*); good-quality vegetable stock powder

dried herbs and spices that you like, including basil, tarragon, rosemary, oregano, cumin, paprika, ground coriander, ground ginger, cayenne, hot chili flakes, turmeric (*herbs and spices should be kept in a dark place; use them within a year or replace them*)

Oils and Vinegars

vegetable oil
olive oil (*regular olive oil for cooking; good-quality extra-virgin olive oil for recipes where you want the olive oil taste to enhance the dish; a mid-range olive oil to use in salad dressings*)
sesame oil
red and white wine vinegar
regular white vinegar
rice vinegar
balsamic vinegar (*an inexpensive one for salad dressings and pastas; an aged one for sprinkling on vegetables and poultry before serving*)

Pasta, Rice, Grains and Beans

long-grain rice
risotto rice (*Carnaroli, Vialone Nano or Arborio*)
brown rice (*for the nutritionally correct*)
dried pasta (*in various long and short shapes*)
cornmeal
lentils
barley
couscous
bulgur

buckwheat

dried beans (*such as black beans, kidney beans, white beans and chickpeas; they should keep years if stored in an airtight container*)

Canned Goods

salmon
tuna
jams and jellies
peanut butter
anchovies
canned chicken and beef broth (*buy low-salt broths*)
canned tomatoes (*San Marzano or other Italian plum tomatoes are the best*)
tomato sauce (*in a jar*)
tomato paste
salsa
olives
marinated artichokes (*to throw into a quiche or omelette*)
canned kidney beans, white beans, black beans and chickpeas

Dried Goods

sun-dried tomatoes
dried mushrooms (*shiitake, porcini*)
dried fruits (*raisins, cranberries, apricots, dates*)
nuts (*keep these in the freezer to stop them from going rancid*)

Baking Ingredients

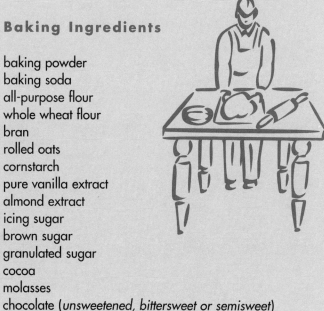

baking powder
baking soda
all-purpose flour
whole wheat flour
bran
rolled oats
cornstarch
pure vanilla extract
almond extract
icing sugar
brown sugar
granulated sugar
cocoa
molasses
chocolate (*unsweetened, bittersweet or semisweet*)
corn syrup
liquid honey

CHOPPING TERMS

dice: cut into ¼-inch cubes

chop: cut into small, even-sized pieces

finely chop: chop as finely as possible

julienne: cut into matchstick-sized pieces

shred: cut into long slivers

Recipes from the Store Cupboard

Quick dishes that can likely be made from ingredients you already have on hand:

Instant Mediterranean Tuna Salad (page 52)

Pasta with Tangy Tomato Sauce (page 120)

Noodles with Spicy Peanut Sauce (page 128)

Chickpea and Caramelized Onion Couscous
    (page 137)

Braised Lentils (page 140)

HOW TO CHOP AN ONION

This is a basic kitchen procedure feared by many because of the effect onion fumes have on your eyes. The best way to avoid crying (other than a gas mask) is to use a very sharp knife that slices through the onion easily, preventing the juices from running out.

Peel the onion.

Cut the onion in half through the root. The root will hold each half together.

Lay the flat surface of the onion half on a cutting board.

With a sharp chef's knife, slice horizontally to the root, but not through it, three or four times. If you don't cut through the root, the onion will hold together.

With the tip of the chef's knife, cut several vertical slices down through the onion.

Holding the onion steady with your knuckles, use the heel of the knife to firmly slice down several times at right angles to the previously made cuts.

CHAPTER 2

Appetizers and Soups

No person in the world has more courage than the person who can stop after eating one peanut.
— Channing Pollock

RUSSIAN MUSHROOM CAVIAR

Many Russians can't afford real caviar so they make mock caviar with finely chopped vegetables. This mushroom caviar looks like the real thing and has a subtle, interesting flavor. Serve with pita toasts and traditional caviar accompaniments if you wish—small bowls of chopped onion, sour cream and grated egg. It will keep, refrigerated, for about a week. You can use regular cultivated mushrooms if desired, but portobello mushrooms give the darkest, most caviar-like look.

2 tbsp olive oil	pinch cayenne
1 onion, chopped	2 tsp lemon juice
1½ lb portobello mushrooms, trimmed and coarsely chopped	2 tbsp chopped fresh dill
3 cloves garlic, chopped	Salt and freshly ground pepper to taste
	. . . . .

Heat 1 tbsp oil in large skillet over medium heat. Add onion and sauté until golden, about 5 to 6 minutes.

Add remaining oil and raise heat to medium-high. Add mushrooms and garlic and sauté until all the mushroom liquid evaporates and the mixture is dry, about 10 to 12 minutes. Remove from heat.

Combine onion and mushroom mixture in food processor and process until minced but not pureed.

Combine the minced mixture with cayenne, lemon juice, dill, salt and pepper in a bowl. Mix well and adjust seasonings to taste. Refrigerate until ready to serve.

PITA TOASTS

Combine 2 tbsp olive oil with 2 tsp sesame oil. Brush on 4 rounds of pita bread. Cut each round into 8 triangles and place on a greased baking sheet.

Bake at 400 F for 6 to 8 minutes or until browned and crisp.

Makes 32 triangles.

WHITE BEAN AND ROASTED GARLIC SPREAD

SERVES 8

This is a great dip to serve with pre-dinner drinks. It can be prepared up to three days ahead of time. Roasted garlic is subtle and mellow. Many gourmet shops sell it, but it is easy to prepare yourself.

2 heads roasted garlic	1/3 cup olive oil
1 19-oz (540 mL) can white beans, drained and rinsed	2 tbsp lemon juice
1/2 tsp ground cumin	pinch cayenne or to taste
1 tsp paprika	3 tbsp chopped parsley
	Salt and freshly ground pepper to taste

Place garlic and beans in food processor or blender. Sprinkle with cumin, paprika, olive oil, lemon juice and cayenne. Process until smooth. If too thick, add a little water.

Stir in parsley, salt and pepper.

ROASTING GARLIC

Cut tops from 2 whole heads of garlic to expose cloves. Remove any flaky skin, but do not peel.

Place garlic in foil and sprinkle with 2 tbsp olive oil. Wrap and bake at 400 F for 35 to 45 minutes or until soft and golden.

Remove garlic from skins by pressing from base of cloves.

Makes about 1/4 cup puree.

FRITTERED ARTICHOKES WITH TAPENADE DIP

You can use corn, cauliflower, oysters, shrimp or leftover cooked vegetables for these crispy fritters. The flour and cornstarch batter clings to the ingredients and results in crisp fritters. These can be reheated in a 350 F oven for 5 minutes, although they will not be quite as crisp.
Tapenade is a paste made with black olives, anchovies, garlic and capers. Use store-bought or homemade.

½ cup all-purpose flour

2 tbsp cornstarch

½ tsp baking powder

Salt and freshly ground pepper to taste

1 egg, beaten

⅓ cup cold water

2 cups chopped canned or roasted artichokes, drained

½ cup chopped onion

½ cup grated Asiago or Parmesan cheese

· · · · ·

TAPENADE DIP

2 tbsp tapenade

½ cup mayonnaise

2 tbsp water

¼ cup chopped parsley

· · · · ·

Vegetable oil for frying

Sift together flour, cornstarch, baking powder, salt and pepper. Make a well in center and add egg and water. Slowly stir into flour mixture. Stir in artichokes, onion and cheese.

Combine tapenade, mayonnaise, water and parsley in separate bowl.

Heat ½ inch of oil in skillet on medium-high heat until a cube of bread turns brown in 15 seconds.

Drop batter into oil by the level tablespoon and cook until golden-brown, about 1 minute per side. Drain and serve with tapenade dip.

FRYING TIP

When frying in oil, use two implements to turn the ingredients. This safety measure prevents food from dropping back into the oil and spattering.

MARINATED FETA CHEESE

SERVES 10

This will keep for up to three weeks in the refrigerator. To preserve, place the cheese in a jar and cover with olive oil. Remove from oil before serving and serve with olives and pita or tortilla chips.

1 lb feta cheese	½ tsp hot red pepper flakes
2 tbsp chopped fresh oregano or 2 tsp dried	1 tsp whole peppercorns
3 tbsp chopped fresh mint or 1 tbsp dried	½ cup olive oil

Cut feta into 1-inch cubes. Place in bowl. Sprinkle with oregano, mint, hot pepper flakes and peppercorns and toss with olive oil. Marinate overnight.

FETA

Greece produces the finest and best-known feta, although this cheese has its origins in countries throughout the eastern Mediterranean, and it is now made in North America, too. The crumbly cheese is made from flavorful sheep's or goat's milk, and is pickled in a saltwater brine. The brine stops the ripening process, keeping the feta young and giving it a sharp, salty flavor.

LAYERED BRIE

SERVES 12

Buy ready-made pesto or make your own. Use inexpensive Brie rather than the pricy French variety in this recipe, or you can use Camembert. (You can also use small wheels of Brie and adjust the amount of filling.)

I sometimes serve this without baking—it looks and tastes great. Serve it with crackers and fruit.

1 2-lb wheel Brie	2 tbsp lemon juice
1 cup sun-dried tomatoes	Freshly ground pepper to taste
2 tbsp olive oil	½ cup pesto

Freeze Brie for 1 hour to firm it.

Preheat oven to 350 F.

Cover tomatoes with hot water. Soak for 30 minutes. Drain well.

Place tomatoes in food processor and chop. Add olive oil and lemon juice and process until pureed. Season with pepper.

Cut Brie in half horizontally with sharp knife. Spread bottom with pesto to ¼ inch from edge. Dot with sun-dried tomato mixture.

Cover with top of Brie and press together to sandwich layers.

Bake for 10 minutes just to soften cheese.

EGGPLANT TORTINO

An excellent fast dish for a party, especially if you use storebought grilled eggplant.

Place a layer of grilled eggplant in bottom of a shallow baking dish. Combine goat cheese and pesto and sprinkle on eggplant. Top with second layer of eggplant. Add second layer of goat cheese and pesto and finish with eggplant.

Pour tomato sauce over eggplant and sprinkle with Parmesan. Bake at 375 F for 20 minutes or until bubbling.

PEPPER-DUSTED CHEDDAR COINS

A savory cheese round perfect as a base for canapes or smoked salmon but also good on its own as a nibbly. Sprinkle on as much black pepper as you like—I like a lot.

1/2 cup butter, at room temperature	pinch cayenne
2 1/2 cups grated old Cheddar cheese	1/4 tsp salt
2 tbsp Dijon mustard	2 tbsp coarsely ground black pepper
1 1/4 cups all-purpose flour	. . . . .

Cream butter in food processor or blender until soft and fluffy. Add cheese and mustard and process until well combined.

Mix together flour, cayenne, salt and 1/2 tsp pepper in bowl. Add cheese mixture and combine just until it holds together. Do not overmix.

Divide dough into 2 portions and roll each into cylinder about 1 inch in diameter. Wrap in plastic and chill in refrigerator for 30 minutes.

Preheat oven to 375 F.

Cut cylinders into slices 1/4 inch thick and lay on ungreased baking sheet. Sprinkle cookies with remaining coarsely ground pepper.

Bake on middle shelf of oven for 10 to 15 minutes or until pale gold. Remove to wire rack. Serve warm or cold.

PROSCIUTTO-WRAPPED PUFF PASTRY

MAKES ABOUT 50 STICKS

You can also wrap the pastry with paper-thin slices of cheese, smoked ham or smoked salmon. For an even easier version, buy prepared cheese straws, cut them in half and wrap.

½ 14-oz (400g) package frozen puff pastry, defrosted

1 egg, beaten with pinch of salt

½ tsp coarsely ground pepper

½ cup grated Parmesan cheese

Salt to taste

12 thin slices prosciutto

· · · · ·

Preheat oven to 400 F.

Roll puff pastry into 12 x 8-inch rectangle. Brush with beaten egg.

Combine pepper, Parmesan and salt and sprinkle over pastry. Cut pastry into ½-inch strips, then cut each strip into 4-inch lengths. Place on baking sheet.

Bake for 10 minutes or until puffed and golden. Cool.

Cut each slice of prosciutto into 4 strips and wrap one strip around each cheese stick.

MEDITERRANEAN PHYLLO CIGARS

Cigars have made a big comeback. Try this non-tobacco vegetarian version for eye appeal and taste. The filling can also be served as a side dish with lamb or pork.

These can be baked ahead and frozen. To reheat, bake at 375 F from the frozen state for 7 to 10 minutes or until the filling is hot.

Salt	pinch cayenne
1 large eggplant, peeled and diced	4 canned tomatoes, chopped
3 tbsp olive oil	2 tbsp lemon juice
3 cloves garlic, chopped	2 tbsp chopped parsley
1/2 tsp ground cumin	Salt to taste
1/2 tsp paprika	7 sheets phyllo pastry
	1/3 cup butter, melted

Salt eggplant lightly and leave in colander for 30 minutes to drain out bitter juice. Pat dry.

Heat oil in large skillet on medium heat. Add eggplant and sauté for about 5 minutes or until beginning to turn golden.

Add garlic, cumin, paprika and cayenne and sauté until spices are absorbed by eggplant, about 1 minute.

Add tomatoes and stir together. Reduce heat to low and continue to cook and stir occasionally until mixture forms a thick mass, about 20 to 30 minutes.

Sprinkle with lemon juice and parsley and stir together. Season with salt.

Preheat oven to 375 F. Arrange phyllo sheets on counter and cover with tea towel. Place one sheet on counter and brush with butter. Cut sheet lengthwise into thirds.

Place about 1 scant tbsp eggplant filling on bottom third of phyllo. Roll up into a cigar shape, leaving ends open. Brush with butter. Repeat with remaining phyllo and eggplant.

Place on buttered baking sheet. Bake for 15 to 20 minutes or until pastry is golden.

POT STICKERS

A tasty and practical little hors d'oeuvre. Make them ahead and reheat them or even freeze them uncooked and cook from the frozen state. Although they may appear to be finicky, they take no time at all. Use ground pork, turkey or veal, or grind up shrimp or salmon for a tasty difference. Quantities are not written in stone in this recipe—add or subtract tastes as you wish. Cook a little filling and adjust the seasonings before assembling.
Serve these with Soy Ginger Dipping Sauce.

1/3 cup chopped cooked spinach	1/2 tsp sesame oil
2 green onions, finely chopped	Salt and freshly ground pepper to taste
8 oz ground pork, chicken or turkey	2 tbsp chopped fresh coriander
2 tsp grated ginger	30 wonton or dumpling wrappers
1 tbsp soy sauce	1 egg white, beaten, optional
1/4 tsp Asian chili sauce or to taste	1 tbsp vegetable oil
1/4 tsp granulated sugar	3/4 cup water

Combine spinach, onions, pork, ginger, soy sauce, chili sauce, sugar and sesame oil by hand or in food processor. Season with salt and pepper and stir in coriander.

Brush edges of wrappers with egg white or water. Place about 1 heaping teaspoon filling in center of each wrapper. Bring corners up to meet and pinch edges together.

Heat vegetable oil in non-stick skillet over medium-high heat. Add dumplings so they are touching each other and cook until bottoms are pale gold, about 1 minute. Pour in water and bring to boil. Cover pan and steam dumplings until firm to touch, about 3 to 4 minutes.

Uncover and cook until water evaporates. Place on serving dish and serve with dip.

SOY GINGER DIPPING SAUCE

Combine 2 tbsp grated ginger, 1/3 cup red wine vinegar, 2 tbsp soy sauce and 1 tsp Asian chili sauce (optional).

Makes about 1/2 cup.

HOT HERBED NUTS

MAKES 4 CUPS

Walnuts or macadamias are good substitutes for the pecans. The nuts should keep for three weeks in an airtight container.

⅓ cup olive oil	2 tsp paprika
4 cups pecans	Salt to taste
2 tbsp dried rosemary	½ tsp cayenne or to taste

Heat oil in large skillet on medium heat. Add pecans, rosemary, paprika, salt and cayenne. Cook, stirring, for 5 minutes or until nuts are browned. Cool.

SPICED CHICKPEAS

Drain 19-oz (540 mL) can of chickpeas and combine with 2 tbsp chili powder, 1 tsp ground cumin, 1 tsp paprika and ¼ cup vegetable oil to coat.

Spread on baking sheet and bake at 350 F for 40 to 45 minutes, shaking the pan occasionally, or until the chickpeas are slightly brown and crunchy.

Makes 2 cups.

THE BEST CHICKEN SOUP

SERVES 4

Look for plump, yellow-skinned capons or pullets (old laying hens)—not anemic-looking, skinny birds—to make a rich broth. Don't add salt until after the soup is cooked. If the chicken has any taste left, use it in chicken salads or pot pies.

Use the soup, unsalted, as a stock base for other soups and sauces.

1 capon or pullet, about 5 lb, cut in 8 pieces	4 sprigs parsley
2 onions, cut in chunks	1 bay leaf
3 carrots, cut in chunks	1 clove garlic
3 stalks celery, cut in chunks	Salt and freshly ground pepper to taste

Cover chicken with cold water by about 1 inch in large pot. Bring to boil. Skim off scum with slotted spoon.

Add onions, carrots, celery, parsley, bay leaf and garlic.

Reduce heat and simmer gently for 3 to 4 hours or until soup is full of flavor. Add salt and pepper to taste. Strain, chill and remove fat.

MEXICAN-STYLE CHICKEN SOUP

To 6 cups chicken soup, add ½ tsp finely chopped jalapeño pepper, 2 cups shredded cooked chicken and 1 small diced avocado. Heat until hot. Season with salt and pepper to taste.

Slice 5 corn tortillas in strips and fry in ¼-inch oil on high heat for 30 seconds or until crisp.

Ladle soup into bowls, season with lime juice and garnish with chopped fresh coriander and tortilla strips.

Serves 4.

GREEK-STYLE CHICKEN SOUP

To 6 cups chicken soup, add 1 tbsp chopped fresh dill and ⅓ cup uncooked long-grain rice. Bring to boil. Simmer on low heat until rice is tender, about 20 minutes. Remove from heat. Slowly whisk in 3 beaten eggs. Season with lots of lemon juice and salt and pepper to taste. Scatter with dill before serving.

Serves 4.

SWEET POTATO AND PEAR SOUP

SERVES 6

A good soup for Christmas or Thanksgiving dinner. The sweeter the pears, the more heat and acid you need to balance the taste.

2 tbsp butter	1 tsp paprika
1 cup chopped onion	5 cups chicken stock
¼ cup chopped carrot	¼ cup whipping cream, optional
¼ cup chopped celery	2 tsp maple syrup or to taste
2 large sweet potatoes, peeled and diced	4 tsp lime juice or to taste
1 pear, peeled and diced	Salt and freshly ground pepper to taste
½ tsp dried thyme	. . . . .

Heat butter in pot on medium heat. Add onion, carrot and celery and sauté for 1 minute.

Add sweet potatoes, pear and thyme and sauté for 2 minutes. Add paprika and chicken stock. Bring to boil. Lower heat and simmer for 15 minutes or until sweet potato is soft.

Puree soup in blender or food processor until smooth. Return to pot. Add cream, maple syrup and lime juice. Simmer for 5 minutes. Season with salt and pepper and add more syrup or lime juice if needed.

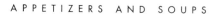

ROASTED TOMATO SOUP

SERVES 4

Roasting tomatoes adds flavor, particularly when tomatoes are not at their best. Roast them and store them, refrigerated, for up to two weeks. Use them in sauces, or mix with other roasted vegetables such as zucchini and eggplant. You can roast any kind of tomato, but plum tomatoes work well because of their thicker skins. For a fast first course, fill with mozzarella cheese, bake until the cheese melts and place on top of a salad.

8 plum tomatoes, halved	1 tsp chili powder
6 cherry tomatoes, halved	1 3-inch strip orange rind
1 onion, thickly sliced	3 cups chicken stock or water
1 red pepper, halved	1/4 hot pepper sauce or to taste
1 tbsp olive oil	Salt and freshly ground pepper to taste
1 tbsp red wine vinegar	8 fresh basil leaves

Preheat oven to 450 F. Place plum and cherry tomatoes, onion and red pepper in bowl and toss with oil and vinegar. Place on baking sheet and bake for 20 minutes or until vegetables are browned.

Peel charred skin off red pepper and chop coarsely. Place plum tomatoes, onion, red pepper, chili powder and orange rind in soup pot on medium heat.

Add stock. Bring to boil and simmer for 10 minutes or until vegetables are tender. Remove orange rind.

Add soup to food processor or blender and puree until smooth. Season with hot pepper sauce, salt and pepper.

Reheat when needed. Garnish with cherry tomatoes and basil leaves.

ROASTED TOMATOES

Preheat oven to 450 F. Cut tomatoes in half and place cut side down on oiled baking sheet. Roast for 20 to 30 minutes depending on size and juiciness. Tomato skin should be slightly brown and cracked.

ROASTED SQUASH SOUP WITH MUSHROOMS

SERVES 6

I tasted this outstanding soup in Brittany in a small restaurant in the middle of the country-side. They included a poached egg on top of each portion, which you could do if you wanted to serve this as a complete meal. Pancetta is Italian cured bacon made from belly pork. Roasting the squash gives the soup a more intense flavor.

3 tbsp olive oil	¼ cup whipping cream
1 large squash, halved and seeded	Salt and freshly ground pepper to taste
1 onion, chopped	6 thin slices pancetta or bacon, diced
1 clove garlic, chopped	4 oz mixed wild mushrooms, thickly sliced
1 tsp chopped fresh thyme or pinch dried	1 clove garlic, finely chopped
pinch cayenne	2 tbsp chopped parsley
5 cups chicken stock	• • • • •

Preheat oven to 450 F.

Place squash on oiled baking sheet, cut side down. Roast for 20 to 30 minutes until squash is soft. Scrape flesh from skin (you should have about 4 cups).

Heat 1 tbsp oil in soup pot on medium-high heat. Add onion and garlic and sauté for 2 minutes or until softened.

Add thyme, cayenne, squash and chicken stock. Bring to boil and simmer for 15 minutes or until vegetables are soft.

Puree soup in food processor until smooth. Return to pot, stir in cream and taste for seasoning, adding salt and pepper as needed. Reheat when needed.

Heat remaining 1 tbsp oil in skillet on medium-high heat and fry pancetta until crisp, about 2 minutes. Remove pancetta and reserve. Pour out all but 1 tbsp fat. Add mushrooms and garlic to skillet and sauté until browned and juice has evaporated, about 5 minutes. Stir in parsley.

Serve soup garnished with pancetta and mushrooms.

IRISH POTATO AND SPINACH SOUP

SERVES 4

Although today's Irish cooking is lighter than the heavy, starchy food of the past, two continuing favorites are potatoes and bacon. They star in this contemporary soup.

2 tbsp butter

1 large onion, sliced

1 lb potatoes, preferably Yukon Gold, peeled and sliced

1 bunch spinach, cleaned, or 1 package frozen spinach, defrosted

4 cups chicken stock

¼ cup whipping cream, optional

Salt and freshly ground pepper to taste

2 oz diced cooked bacon

½ cup chopped chives

· · · · ·

Heat butter in soup pot on medium-high heat. Add onion and potatoes and sauté for 2 minutes. Reduce heat, cover and simmer for 10 minutes.

Add spinach and chicken stock to pot and bring to boil. Simmer for 10 minutes or until potatoes are very soft.

Puree soup in food processor or blender until smooth. Return to pot and add a little more stock if soup is too thick.

Add cream and bring to boil. Season with salt and pepper. Garnish with bacon and chives.

PARSNIP, CARROT AND MAPLE SOUP

SERVES 6

This creamy root vegetable soup has a hint of maple, which balances the curry flavor.

2 tbsp butter	$1/2$ tsp grated nutmeg
1 lb carrots, peeled and chopped	1 tbsp lemon juice or to taste
1 lb parsnips, peeled and chopped	Salt and pepper to taste
1 onion, chopped	• • • • •
1 tsp grated ginger	MINT MAPLE CREAM
1 tsp curry powder	$1/4$ cup sour cream
5 cups chicken stock or water	1 tbsp maple syrup
2 tbsp maple syrup	1 tbsp chopped fresh mint
$1/4$ cup whipping cream	• • • • •

Heat butter in large pot on low heat. Add carrots, parsnips, onion, ginger and curry powder. Coat with butter, cover and cook gently for 10 minutes, or until vegetables are slightly softened.

Pour in stock, bring to boil, cover and simmer gently for 20 minutes, or until vegetables are very soft.

Puree soup in blender or food processor until smooth. Pour soup back into pot.

Add maple syrup, cream, nutmeg, lemon juice, salt and pepper. Simmer for 5 minutes. Taste for seasoning, adding more lemon juice or maple syrup if needed.

Beat together sour cream, maple syrup and mint. Serve soup garnished with swirl of cream.

STOCK

Most people do not make homemade stock any-more. Use good-quality stock cubes or canned low-salt chicken broth diluted with double the amount of water called for. You can also buy ready-made chicken soup or stock at supermarkets or gourmet grocery stores.

ROASTED CORN AND SWEET POTATO CHOWDER

SERVES 4 TO 6

If you are using fresh corn, you'll need four ears for 2 cups kernels. Using a sharp knife, slice kernels off cob into bowl, saving any juice. You can also use defrosted frozen corn. Dice vegetables the same size for even cooking and an attractive look. Serve with Eggplant Sandwiches (page 38) for a hearty vegetarian meal.

2 cups corn kernels	1 tsp chili powder
1 tbsp olive oil	5 cups chicken or vegetable stock
1 onion, chopped	1/2 tsp hot pepper sauce
2 cloves garlic, chopped	1 bay leaf
1/2 red pepper, diced	Salt and freshly ground pepper to taste
1/2 green pepper, diced	1/2 cup sour cream
1 large sweet potato, peeled and diced	1/4 cup chopped fresh coriander

Preheat oven to 450 F.

Place corn on baking sheet and roast in oven for 10 minutes, stirring occasionally. When corn is browned, remove to bowl.

Heat oil in large pot on medium-high heat. Add onion and sauté until soft and slightly browned, about 5 minutes.

Add garlic, red and green pepper, sweet potato and chili powder. Sauté for 1 minute.

Pour in chicken stock and hot pepper sauce, bring to boil, then simmer for 10 minutes. Add corn and bay leaf and simmer for 5 minutes or until vegetables are tender. Remove bay leaf and season with salt and pepper.

Combine sour cream and coriander. Ladle soup into bowls and streak with cream.

VEGETABLE STOCK

Combine equal amounts of onion, carrots and celery. Toss in a few garlic cloves and some parsley stalks. (You can also add well-washed mushroom stems, leek tops, potato skins, pea pods and peelings and ends from other vegetables.

Add water to cover, bring to a boil, reduce heat and simmer gently for 1 1/2 hours. Strain and use stock in soups and sauces. It should keep refrigerated for 5 days or frozen for up to 3 months.

EGYPTIAN LENTIL SOUP

SERVES 4

I tasted this fabulous lentil soup in Cairo and came home with the recipe.

1 tbsp olive oil

1 onion, finely chopped

1 clove garlic, finely chopped

1 tsp ground ginger

2 tsp ground cumin

2 tsp dried ground coriander

1 cup dried red lentils, rinsed

4 to 5 cups chicken stock or water

2 slices lemon

1/2 cup chopped canned tomatoes

1/4 tsp cayenne or to taste

Salt and freshly ground pepper to taste

3 tbsp chopped fresh coriander

. . . . .

Heat oil in heavy pot on medium-high heat. Sauté onion and garlic until softened, about 2 minutes.

Stir in ginger, cumin and coriander and sauté for 1 minute. Stir in lentils and cook for 1 minute or until coated with spices.

Add 4 cups stock, lemon slices, tomatoes and cayenne. Bring to boil, reduce heat, cover and simmer for about 45 minutes or until lentils are tender. Add more stock if needed.

Discard lemon slices and puree soup in blender or food processor. Season with salt and pepper. Sprinkle with fresh coriander.

SORREL AND HERB SOUP

SERVES 4

Sorrel is a leafy vegetable that looks like bright-green spinach, but it has an intensely lemony flavor. It is also wonderful in salsas.

You can use any fresh herbs in this soup. My choice is just a guideline. This is a perfect springtime soup—light, fragrant, tasty and good hot or chilled.

2 tbsp butter	4 cups chicken stock
1 cup finely chopped onion	Salt and freshly ground pepper to taste
1/2 cup finely chopped celery	pinch granulated sugar
2 cups slivered fresh sorrel or spinach	1 tbsp lemon juice or to taste
2 tbsp finely chopped chives	1/4 cup crumbled goat cheese
2 tbsp finely chopped fresh mint	2 tbsp chopped chives
1 tbsp finely chopped fresh tarragon	• • • • •

Melt butter in large pot on low heat. When it sizzles, add onion and celery. Cook for 5 minutes or until softened.

Add sorrel, chives, mint, tarragon, chicken stock, salt, pepper and sugar. Cover and simmer for 15 minutes. Add lemon juice—the soup should be fairly tart.

Ladle soup into bowls and sprinkle with goat cheese and chives.

PASTA E FAGIOLI

SERVES 4

Not a traditional method of making this soup/stew, but a fast version that is full of taste. Omit the garlic cloves if you don't like their mellow flavor, but they do give depth to the finished product. If you are using leftover long pasta, cut it into small pieces before adding to the soup.

12 garlic cloves, unpeeled	3 cups chicken stock or water
3 tbsp olive oil	2 cups cooked short pasta
½ onion, chopped	Salt and freshly ground pepper to taste
¼ cup chopped celery	¼ cup chopped parsley
1 cup chopped canned tomatoes	Grated Parmesan cheese
1 19-oz (540 mL) can white kidney beans, drained and rinsed	. . . . .

Bring small pot of water to boil. Add garlic cloves and boil for 5 minutes or until softened. Remove skins.

Heat oil in soup pot on medium heat. Add garlic and sauté for 3 minutes or until tinged with gold.

Add onion and celery and sauté for 2 minutes or until slightly softened.

Stir in tomatoes and cook for 10 minutes. Add beans and cook for 5 minutes

Add stock and pasta and cook for 5 minutes or until pasta is heated through. Season well with salt and pepper.

Stir in parsley and serve with grated Parmesan.

QUICK MISO SOUP WITH SPINACH AND NOODLES

SERVES 2

Dashi is a stock made from dried kelp and dried bonito flakes. Buy it in powdered form at a Japanese grocery store or health food shop and follow the package directions to make the stock. Use chicken stock if dashi is unavailable.

4 cups dashi or chicken stock	3 tbsp white or red miso
2 cups diced tofu	2 cups cooked noodles
2 cups chopped baby spinach or watercress leaves	3 green onions, chopped
	· · · · ·

Bring stock to simmer in pot and add tofu and spinach. Simmer for 1 minute.

Combine miso with a little stock, then stir back into soup.

Place noodles in 2 bowls. Top with soup and garnish with green onions.

MISO

Miso is essentially a Japanese fermented soybean paste. It has a unique taste—slightly salty and fragrant—as well as important medicinal properties. It is high in protein, amino acids, vitamins, minerals and very low in calories and fat.

The Japanese have always regarded miso as a health food and cancer fighter. Today it and other soy-based foods are being studied for how their natural estrogen content can help menopausal problems.

Try light (usually yellow) miso in salad dressings instead of oil or to add flavor to soups, sauces or vegetables. Darker red or brown miso combines well with hearty soups, vegetables and lentil dishes.

SPICY VIETNAMESE BEEF SOUP

SERVES 4

To make authentic Vietnamese beef soup or pho, *you need to start with a spiced beef stock made from oxtails and other meats. I simplify the dish by starting with either low-salt canned beef broth or good-quality stock cubes, simmered with spices and vegetables for 30 minutes.*

Serve this as an easy supper dish or a filling lunch. Place the garnishes in bowls and have people garnish their own soup. To make sure the beef is very thinly sliced, freeze it for 20 minutes before slicing. The hot soup cooks the beef.

8 cups beef stock	2 cups bean sprouts
4 star anise or ½ tsp fennel seeds	8 oz sirloin tip, thinly sliced
1-inch piece cinnamon stick	• • • • •
4 slices ginger, smashed	GARNISH
3 whole cloves	Sprigs fresh mint and coriander
1 onion, coarsely chopped	2 chili peppers, thinly sliced,
2 carrots, coarsely chopped	or Asian chili sauce
1 stalk celery, coarsely chopped	1 lime, thinly sliced
2 tbsp Thai fish sauce or soy sauce	1 cup bean sprouts
12 oz rice noodles	3 green onions, thinly sliced
1 onion, thinly sliced	• • • • •

Place stock, star anise, cinnamon, ginger, cloves, chopped onion, carrots, celery and fish sauce in soup pot. Bring to boil and simmer for 30 minutes. Strain.

Soak rice noodles in hot water for 30 minutes. Drain in colander and reserve.

Bring strained stock to boil. Divide rice noodles among 4 bowls. Top with sliced onion, bean sprouts and meat.

Pour boiling soup into bowls and serve immediately. Place garnishes in bowls and serve with soup.

HOT AND SOUR SHRIMP SOUP

SERVES 4

This soup is hot, sour and salty. Add vinegar, hot sauce and soy sauce until the tastes are balanced to your liking.

4 dried Chinese or fresh shiitake mushrooms	pinch granulated sugar
1/2 cup rice noodles	2 tbsp soy sauce
4 cups chicken stock	1/2 tsp sesame oil
1 tbsp grated ginger	1 egg, slightly beaten
8 shrimp, shelled	Salt and freshly ground pepper to taste
1 tbsp rice vinegar	2 tbsp chopped fresh coriander
1 tsp Asian chili sauce	2 green onions, slivered

Soak dried mushrooms and rice noodles in hot water for 20 minutes. Rinse and drain. Slice mushrooms.

Combine mushrooms, stock and ginger in soup pot. Bring to boil and simmer for 5 minutes.

Add noodles, shrimp, vinegar, chili sauce, sugar, soy sauce and sesame oil. Simmer for 2 minutes.

Stir in egg. Season with salt and pepper. Just before serving, stir in coriander and green onions.

ASIAN CHILI SAUCES

My favorite is *sambal oelek*, an Indonesian chili sauce. It is pure chili with a little added vinegar, and it has the freshest taste. The Thai and Vietnamese chili sauces, also called *sriracha*, usually have vinegar, sugar and sometimes garlic added to them.

SPICED GAZPACHO

SERVES 6

Serve with crispy pappadums. Use a whole jalapeño with seeds for a searing taste.

3 large fresh tomatoes, seeded and quartered, about 5 cups

2 cups chopped red or Spanish onion

1 green pepper, chopped

2 cups peeled and chopped seedless cucumber

2 cloves garlic, chopped

1 tsp chopped jalapeño pepper or to taste

2 tbsp olive oil

2 cups tomato juice

½ cup red wine

3 tbsp red wine vinegar

Salt and freshly ground pepper to taste

Hot pepper sauce to taste

· · · · ·

GARNISH

½ cup chopped cucumber

¼ cup chopped onion

2 tbsp chopped fresh coriander

Croutons

· · · · ·

Combine tomatoes, onion, green pepper, cucumber, garlic and jalapeño in food processor. Process until chunky and remove to bowl.

Stir in olive oil, tomato juice, wine and vinegar. Thin with a little water if necessary.

Season well with salt, pepper and hot pepper sauce. Chill.

Garnish with chopped cucumber, onion, coriander and croutons.

CHILLED CUCUMBER AND MINT SOUP

SERVES 6

A cold summer soup that looks pretty served in glass mugs or bowls. Chilling dulls flavor, so reseason the soup before serving. Garnish with thin cucumber slices, chopped chives and cooked baby shrimp, if desired.

1 seedless cucumber	1 cup buttermilk
3 leeks, trimmed and chopped	2 tbsp chopped fresh mint
2 cloves garlic, chopped	1 tbsp lime juice
4 cups chicken stock	Salt and freshly ground pepper to taste

Peel strips off cucumber about ½ inch wide, leaving some skin intact. Slice cucumber into rounds.

Combine cucumber, leeks, garlic and stock in soup pot. Bring to boil, reduce heat, cover and simmer gently for 20 minutes or until vegetables are cooked.

Puree soup in food processor or blender. Add buttermilk, mint and lime juice. Season with salt and pepper and chill overnight in refrigerator.

CHAPTER 3

Light Dishes

Life is too short to stuff mushrooms.
—Shirley Conran

EGGS ARIZONA STYLE

SERVES 4

Chorizo is a spicy garlic sausage from Spain. Use Polish sausage as a substitute.
   Serve the eggs with Refried Beans (page 141) and fruit slices and top with salsa and sour cream.

1 tbsp olive oil	8 eggs, beaten
1 onion, chopped	2 tbsp sour cream
1 green pepper, chopped	Salt and freshly ground pepper to taste
2 cups chopped chorizo or	4 tortilla baskets or warm tortillas
Polish sausage	3 tbsp chopped fresh coriander

Heat olive oil in skillet on medium-high heat. Add onion, pepper and chorizo. Sauté until onion and pepper are softened and chorizo is browned, about 3 minutes.

Reduce heat to low and add eggs. Mix with other ingredients and stir until lightly scrambled.

Stir in sour cream. Season with salt and pepper. (Eggs should not be dry.)

Spoon eggs into tortilla baskets. Sprinkle with coriander.

TORTILLA BASKETS

Lay 4 small flour tortillas on counter. Brush lightly with oil. Place inside ovenproof bowls or cut into smaller rounds and place inside muffin tins. Bake at 375 F for 8 to 10 minutes or until crisp.

   Store in an airtight container. Do not fill until just before using.

TORTILLAS

Tortillas, a staple of both Mexican and Southwestern cooking, are now outselling bagels, English muffins and pitas combined. They are low-fat, calorie-light and very versatile. They keep well both refrigerated or frozen. Some tortillas are based on corn, but it is the flour types that are flying off the shelves. The best flour tortillas come from Mexican or Latin American shops, they are thinner and tastier than the slightly more glutinous type available in supermarkets.

HUEVOS RANCHEROS

SERVES 2

This is the most popular breakfast item at the Café Pascal in Santa Fe. Serve them with warm tortillas and sour cream.

2 tbsp olive oil	½ tsp dried basil
1 onion, chopped	½ tsp hot red pepper flakes
2 cloves garlic, chopped	Salt and freshly ground pepper to taste
2 cups chopped tomatoes	4 eggs
2 tsp chili powder	. . . . .

Heat olive oil in skillet on medium heat. Add onion and garlic and sauté for 3 minutes or until soft.

Add tomatoes, chili powder, basil and hot pepper flakes.

Simmer for 20 minutes or until thickened. Season with salt and pepper.

Reduce heat to low and break 4 eggs over mixture. Cover pan and simmer for 5 minutes or until eggs are set.

LOW-CHOLESTEROL EGGS

There is a new kind of egg that is lower in cholesterol and higher in omega-3 oils—better for your health. The eggs come from chickens that are fed a special vegetarian diet. They even contain fewer calories!

MY FAVORITE QUESADILLA

SERVES 4

A quesadilla is a Mexican cheese sandwich usually combined or topped with a salsa. The basic quesadilla is made with Monterey Jack cheese and salsa, but your imagination is the limit.

Serve these with a salad as a light supper dish or cut into triangles to serve as a nibbly. They can be made ahead of time and reheated at 350 F for 5 minutes.

2 tbsp olive oil	8 small flour tortillas
2 tbsp wine vinegar	2 cups grated Monterey Jack cheese
2 cloves garlic, chopped	1/4 cup chopped green onions
4 portobello mushrooms	3 tbsp olive oil
Salt and freshly ground pepper to taste	1 cup salsa

Combine 2 tbsp oil, vinegar and garlic and brush on mushrooms. Season with salt and pepper.

Place mushrooms on baking sheet and broil for 3 minutes on each side or until cooked. Slice.

Lay tortillas on counter. Cover one half of each tortilla with mushrooms, cheese and green onions. Fold over.

Heat 2 tsp oil in large non-stick skillet on medium heat. Fry quesadillas, two at a time, for 2 to 3 minutes, covered, until brown. Turn and fry second side, uncovered, for about 2 minutes or until cheese is melted. Keep warm in 200 F oven. Repeat with remaining quesadillas.

Cut quesadillas into wedges and serve with salsa.

HOMEMADE TOMATO SALSA

This salsa keeps for about three days. The riper the tomatoes, the better the result.

Combine 2 tbsp chopped onion, 2 cups coarsely chopped fresh plum tomatoes, 2 finely chopped cloves garlic, 1 tsp finely chopped jalapeño or serrano peppers and the juice of 1 lime.

Makes about 2 cups.

BACON, POTATO AND CHIVE FRITTATA

SERVES 3 TO 4

Smoked Gruyère gives an exceptional flavor to this dish, but regular Gruyère can be substituted. Leftovers make a good sandwich filling the next day. This can also be served cold as picnic food.

1 tbsp vegetable oil	Salt and freshly ground pepper to taste
4 oz bacon, diced	2 tbsp butter
2 Yukon Gold or baking potatoes, peeled and cubed	6 eggs
1 tbsp chopped fresh rosemary or 1 tsp dried	¼ cup whipping cream
	½ cup grated smoked Gruyère cheese
	½ cup chopped chives or green onions

Heat oil in 9-inch ovenproof skillet on medium heat. Sauté bacon until fat begins to release.

Add potatoes and sauté for 2 minutes. Cover pan and cook for 15 minutes or until potatoes are brown and tender.

Sprinkle potatoes with rosemary, salt and pepper. Stir in butter.

Whisk together eggs, cream, cheese and chives in large bowl. Pour over potatoes in skillet, pushing potatoes into egg mixture. Cook until eggs are set, stirring occasionally, about 5 minutes. The top will be slightly liquid.

Preheat broiler and place skillet under it. Broil until top is just set. Turn out onto serving platter and cut in wedges. Serve hot or cold.

PASTA FRITTATA

This is a good way to use up leftover pasta, even if it is mixed with sauce. Combine cooked noodles with ingredients such as chopped prosciutto or smoked turkey, grated cheese (e.g., Parmesan or mozzarella), chopped herbs (parsley or basil) and about 4 to 6 eggs for every 4 cups of pasta. Cook using the same method as the bacon frittata and serve with a salad for a casual supper.

TOMATO SANDWICHES

Soup-and-sandwich suppers are quick and comforting. At our cottage, my husband, Bruce, is the best sandwich maker. His specialty is the following tomato sandwich.

4 ripe tomatoes	8 slices good-quality grainy bread
1/2 cup mayonnaise	2 tbsp olive oil
2 tbsp pesto	Salt and freshly ground pepper to taste

Slice tomatoes thickly.

Combine mayonnaise and pesto.

Spread 4 slices of bread with pesto mayonnaise. Overlap slices of tomato. Drizzle with olive oil and season with lots of salt and pepper. Top with remaining 4 slices of bread. Press down gently.

PORTOBELLO MUSHROOM SANDWICHES

MAKES 4 SANDWICHES

A real treat for vegetarians who crave a meaty taste.

4 portobello mushrooms

¼ cup olive oil

2 tbsp balsamic vinegar

2 cloves garlic, chopped

3 oz goat cheese

¼ cup pesto

8 slices Italian baguette or focaccia

4 leaves Romaine, arugula,

endive or radicchio

Salt and freshly ground pepper to taste

Trim stems from mushrooms. Wipe mushrooms clean with paper towel.

Whisk together olive oil, vinegar and garlic in small bowl. Brush mixture over mushrooms.

Grill or sauté mushrooms for about 3 minutes per side or until softened. Cool and slice thinly.

Mix together goat cheese and pesto. Spread on 4 slices of bread. Top with mushrooms and lettuce. Season with salt and pepper. Complete sandwiches with remaining slices of bread.

MUSHROOM STOCK

Use leftover mushroom stems to make stock. Wash the stems and place in a pot. Cover with water, bring to a boil and simmer for about 30 minutes or until the liquid is reduced by half. Use the mushroom stock in sauces, gravies and soups.

EGGPLANT SANDWICHES

MAKES 4 SANDWICHES

Use focaccia, Calabrese rolls, cornbread or any other firm loaf instead of sourdough. You can substitute pesto for the olive paste—both are sold in jars at Italian grocery stores, gourmet shops and some supermarkets. The sandwiches do not have to be fried, but it does melt the cheese, creating a wonderfully gooey concoction.

1 medium eggplant	2 tomatoes, sliced
3 tbsp olive oil	1 cup grated Asiago cheese
8 slices sourdough bread	pinch hot red pepper flakes, optional
1 clove garlic, halved	12 fresh basil leaves
¼ cup mayonnaise	1 bunch arugula, stemmed
2 tbsp olive paste	Salt and freshly ground pepper to taste

Slice eggplant into slices ¼ inch thick. Brush with 2 tbsp oil. Grill or broil eggplant for about 4 minutes per side or until tender and brown. Cool.

Slice bread in half horizontally. Rub both halves with garlic.

Combine mayonnaise and olive paste. Spread on 4 slices of bread.

Layer eggplant, tomatoes, cheese, hot pepper flakes, basil leaves and arugula on top of mayonnaise. Season with salt and pepper. Place remaining slices of bread on sandwiches and press together.

Heat remaining 1 tbsp oil in non-stick skillet on medium heat. Fry sandwiches lightly for about 1 minute per side or until cheese has melted, pressing down with spatula as sandwiches cook.

THE ULTIMATE GRILLED CHEESE SANDWICH

MAKES 1 SANDWICH

Use unpasteurized raw milk Cheddar if you can find it. Although the bacteria in raw milk cheese may cause problems for some people (e.g., the elderly, pregnant women and those with fragile immune systems), the flavor of the cheese makes this an outstanding sandwich. Add chutney, fried onions, tomato, bacon, pesto or arugula to the sandwich if you wish.

2 tsp butter, at room temperature

2 thick slices egg bread

¼ cup grated old Cheddar cheese, preferably raw milk

Heat skillet on medium-low heat.

Spread butter on one side of each slice of bread. Place cheese plus any additions on unbuttered side of one slice. Add second slice of bread, buttered side out.

Place sandwich in skillet and cook gently for 1 minute on each side, pressing down occasionally to help melt cheese. Bread should be golden-brown and cheese should be melted.

CHICKEN WRAPS

SERVES 6

These make a good lunch sandwich served whole or cut in half. Cut the wraps on the diagonal if you are serving them as hors d'oeuvres.

2 cups diced cooked chicken	1 tbsp lemon juice
4 green onions, chopped	1/4 cup chopped fresh coriander,
1 tsp curry powder	mint or parsley
1 tbsp chutney	Salt and freshly ground pepper to taste
3/4 cup mayonnaise	6 large flour tortillas
2 tbsp plain yogurt	1 bunch fresh spinach, stemmed

Place chicken, green onions, curry powder, chutney, mayonnaise, yogurt, lemon juice and coriander in food processor. Combine until spreadable. Season with salt and pepper.

Spread about 1/2 cup chicken mixture on each tortilla. Top with spinach leaves. Roll up and seal edge with a little chicken spread. Wrap in plastic wrap. Refrigerate for 2 hours or overnight.

Cut into sections and place on platter.

WRAPS

A wrap is a kind of sandwich. The wrappers are usually flour tortillas, although you can use anything that rolls up. The fillings can be hot or cold, and they shouldn't leak out. Wraps are quick to make, easy to handle, and great for people who eat on the run.

TOMATO SANDWICHES (PAGE 36)

CRISPY-SKINNED SALMON WITH CONFIT SPICES (PAGE 58)

HAM, GOAT CHEESE AND ARUGULA WRAPS

SERVES 6

You can substitute smoked ham for prosciutto and a mixture of feta and cream cheese for the goat cheese. Serve as a nibble or as part of a sandwich platter.

12 oz goat cheese	6 large flour tortillas
Pepper to taste	2 bunches arugula, stemmed
3 dried figs, finely chopped	12 oz prosciutto, thinly sliced

Cream goat cheese and season with pepper. Mix in dried figs.

Spread cheese mixture on tortillas to ½ inch of edge. Lay arugula on top. Place prosciutto in one layer over arugula.

Roll up tortillas and seal the open edge with cheese. Wrap in plastic wrap and refrigerate for 2 hours or overnight.

Slice wraps before serving.

MEDITERRANEAN TART

SERVES 8

Substitute grilled red pepper strips for the anchovies, if desired. Defrost frozen puff pastry in the refrigerator for two to three hours or overnight.

1 14-oz (400 g) package puff pastry	Salt and freshly ground pepper to taste
2 tbsp olive oil	1 cup chopped tomatoes
3 large Spanish onions, halved and thinly sliced	1 tsp dried oregano
	6 anchovies, halved lengthwise
1 tbsp balsamic vinegar	8 black olives, pitted and halved
1 tsp dried thyme	1/4 cup grated Parmesan cheese

Roll out pastry and cut into 12 x 8-inch rectangle about 1/8 inch thick. Place on baking sheet. Brush edges with water.

Roll out leftover pastry and cut 2 strips 1/2 inch wide and 12 inches long, and 2 strips 1/2 inch wide and 8 inches long. Lay strips along edges of rectangle. Prick base. Chill for 30 minutes.

Preheat oven to 400 F.

Heat oil in large skillet, on medium heat. Add onions and cook, stirring, for 5 minutes. Cover, reduce heat to medium-low and cook for 15 minutes or until onions are very soft. Remove lid, raise heat and cook until all liquid disappears and onions begin to brown.

Stir in balsamic vinegar and thyme. Cook for 1 minute. Season with salt and pepper. Reserve.

Wipe out pan, add tomatoes and oregano and cook together for 5 minutes or until thickened. Season with salt and pepper.

Spread onions over pastry. Top with tomatoes. Make a lattice pattern with anchovies. Dot lattice with olives. Sprinkle with Parmesan.

Bake for 25 minutes or until pastry is golden.

PHYLLO TART WITH HAM, CHEESE AND SPINACH

SERVES 6

This makes a wonderful light meal simply served with a sliced tomato salad or a spectacular brunch dish.

1 bunch spinach	1 lb frozen phyllo pastry, defrosted
1/4 tsp grated nutmeg	1/3 cup butter, melted
2 eggs	4 oz Black Forest or other smoked
1/2 cup whipping cream	ham, thinly sliced
Salt and freshly ground pepper to taste	2 cups grated Cheddar cheese

Preheat oven to 375 F.

Wash and stem spinach and place in pot just with water clinging to leaves. Cover and cook on medium heat just until wilted, about 5 minutes. Cool under cold water and squeeze dry.

Combine spinach, nutmeg, eggs and whipping cream in large bowl. Season with salt and pepper.

Butter 8-inch baking dish. Line dish with sheet of phyllo, letting excess hang over edges. (You may need 2 sheets to completely cover base and sides of dish.) Lightly brush with melted butter. Continue layering until you have 6 sheets of phyllo.

Layer one-third of ham and cheese on phyllo. Add half of spinach mixture, one-third more ham and cheese, half of spinach, and finish with remaining ham and cheese.

Cut off excess phyllo. Fold in edges and brush with melted butter. Top with sheet of phyllo. Brush lightly with melted butter and repeat with 4 more sheets. Tuck in any edges. Brush top sheet with melted butter.

Bake for 30 to 35 minutes or until phyllo is crisp and filling is hot. Let rest for 10 minutes. Cut into squares to serve.

CHEESE AND CARAMELIZED ONION BREAD PUDDING

SERVES 8

Bread puddings can be prepared ahead of time and baked when needed. Use whatever you have on hand—cooked vegetables, cooked bacon, ham or sausage, and your favorite cheeses (but remember that low-fat cheese just doesn't have enough flavor or texture for this pudding). Add ½ cup milk or cream for each egg (the thicker the cream, the richer the dish). Use thinly sliced bread if you want the bread to disappear in the pudding; use chunks of coarser bread if you want added taste and texture.

Serve this with Maple-glazed Sticky Bacon, a tomato salsa and fresh asparagus or a green bean salad.

2 tbsp olive oil	2 cups grated Cheddar cheese
2 large Spanish onions, thinly sliced	1 tbsp Dijon mustard
2 tsp granulated sugar	1 tsp hot red pepper sauce
2 tbsp balsamic vinegar	6 eggs, beaten
½ tsp dried thyme	3 cups whipping cream, light cream or milk
12 thin slices bread, crusts removed	Salt and pepper to taste

Heat oil in skillet on medium-high heat. Add onions and sauté for 2 to 3 minutes or until beginning to soften. Stir in sugar. Reduce heat to medium-low and sauté until onions become a golden tangle, about 5 to 10 minutes.

Add balsamic vinegar and thyme. Cook for 1 minute.

Layer half of bread slices in buttered 13 x 9-inch baking dish. Top with half of onions and half of cheese. Make a second layer of bread, onions and cheese.

Whisk together mustard, hot pepper sauce, eggs and cream. Season with salt and pepper. Pour over pudding. Let sit for 1 hour or overnight in refrigerator.

Preheat oven to 350 F. Bake pudding for 40 minutes or until puffed and set.

MAPLE-GLAZED STICKY BACON

Place 1 lb bacon on baking sheet. Drizzle 2 tbsp maple syrup over bacon and sprinkle with coarsely ground pepper. Bake for 7 to 10 minutes or until crisp. Drain on paper towels.

Serves 8.

SPICED MUSHROOMS ON COUNTRY BREAD

SERVES 4

A first course as well as a light dinner dish that is easy to prepare but fancy enough to satisfy the most sophisticated guests. Serve surrounded by peppery lettuce such as frisee, radicchio and endive.

3 tbsp olive oil	2 tbsp chopped parsley
1 tbsp chopped garlic	2 tbsp chopped fresh mint or basil
3 large portobello mushrooms, stemmed and thinly sliced	2 tbsp Port or Madeira
1 tsp cracked peppercorns (page 56)	2 tbsp butter
1 tsp cracked coriander seeds	Salt and freshly ground pepper to taste
½ cup chicken or vegetable stock	4 slices country bread, toasted
	• • • • •

Heat oil in skillet on medium-high heat. Add garlic and sauté for 1 minute.

Add mushrooms, peppercorns and coriander seeds. Sauté for 2 to 3 minutes or until mushrooms are softened and exuding liquid.

Stir in stock, parsley and mint. Bring to boil and cook until reduced by half.

Reduce heat and stir in Port and butter. Season well with salt and pepper. Pile on top of toasted bread.

NACHO PIZZA

SERVES 2

A perfect meal for kids—healthy and familiar. Serve with extra sour cream.

1 10-inch prebaked pizza crust
1 cup drained kidney beans
1 cup corn kernels
2 cups grated Cheddar or
Monterey Jack cheese

3 green onions, chopped
1 cup salsa
1/2 cup sour cream
· · · · ·

Preheat oven to 425 F.

Top pizza base with beans, corn, cheese, onions, salsa and sour cream.

Bake for 10 minutes or until cheese bubbles.

WARM CHICKEN SALAD WITH SESAME GINGER DRESSING

SERVES 4

Substitute fish or shellfish for the chicken. Serve for a summer supper or as part of a buffet.

SESAME GINGER DRESSING

2 tbsp soy sauce	4 boneless, skinless single chicken breasts
1/4 cup rice vinegar	2 cups spinach, washed and dried
1 tbsp brown sugar	1 small head Boston lettuce, torn in pieces
1 tbsp grated ginger	3 green onions, slivered
2 tsp Dijon mustard	1 cup watercress leaves
1/4 cup vegetable oil	2 tbsp sesame seeds, preferably black
1 tbsp sesame oil	

Whisk together soy sauce, vinegar, sugar, ginger, mustard, vegetable oil and sesame oil.

Place chicken in dish. Pour 1/4 cup dressing over chicken. Marinate for 30 minutes.

Grill or broil chicken for about 5 minutes per side or until juices run clear. Keep warm.

Combine spinach, lettuce, green onions and watercress in large bowl. Toss with remaining dressing.

Place salad on serving plates and top with warm chicken and any juices. Sprinkle with sesame seeds.

GRILLED ORANGE PORK SALAD WITH CHILI DRESSING

SERVES 4

This is an excellent summer buffet dish.

¼ cup orange juice	1 red onion, sliced in rings
2 tsp grated orange rind	• • • • •
Salt and pepper	CHILI DRESSING
1 tsp Asian chili sauce	1 tsp Asian chili sauce
1 clove garlic, chopped	2 tbsp lime juice
2 tbsp olive oil	¼ cup plain yogurt
1 10-oz pork tenderloin	¼ cup mayonnaise
6 cups lettuce leaves	Salt and freshly ground pepper to taste
1 avocado, diced	• • • • •

Combine orange juice and rind, salt and pepper, chili sauce, garlic and olive oil. Pour over pork and marinate for 30 minutes.

Grill or broil pork on medium heat, turning occasionally, for about 20 minutes or until juices are no longer pink. Cool and slice into thin rounds.

Place lettuce leaves on platter. Arrange pork slices on top. Surround with avocado and red onion rings.

Combine chili sauce, lime juice, yogurt, mayonnaise, salt and pepper for dressing. Thin with a little warm water if necessary. Drizzle half of dressing on salad and pass remainder separately.

GRILLED SQUID SALAD

SERVES 4

A quick recipe for a superb, simple salad to serve before pasta.

8 squid, cleaned and cut in half	2 cloves garlic, finely chopped
⅓ cup olive oil	2 tsp chopped fresh thyme or ½ tsp dried
Salt and freshly ground pepper to taste	8 cups mixed lettuce, including
3 tbsp balsamic vinegar	arugula and radicchio

Score squid in ¼-inch slices with tip of sharp knife, almost all the way through. Brush squid with a little olive oil and season with salt and pepper.

Whisk together remaining olive oil, vinegar, garlic and thyme.

Preheat grill or grill pan to high. Place squid on grill, pressing down with spatula to help them cook as quickly as possible. Grill for 1 to 2 minutes per side, brushing with vinaigrette when you turn them. Remove immediately and place on top of lettuce.

Pour remaining vinaigrette over squid and serve warm.

SQUID

Squid is a relatively inexpensive seafood that does not seem to be altered by freezing. Look for a shiny, firm appearance and a delicate ocean smell. If the squid has not been cleaned, the membrane should be gray; a pink or purple membrane is a sign of age. Smaller squid are usually more tender than large ones.

To clean squid, cut off the head with the tentacles attached. Discard the head and reserve the tentacles. Pull off the gray membrane and discard it. Remove the plastic-like cartilage from the sac. Not a task for the squeamish, but most squid is available already cleaned.

Once the squid has been rinsed, it is ready for cooking. It should be either flash-cooked or slowly simmered to avoid a rubber-tire texture.

SOUTHWESTERN CHICKEN SALAD

SERVES 6

A colorful chicken salad with a little heat in it. Use as many colors of peppers as you can find. Serve with corn chips.

If you don't want to grill whole cobs, defrost 2 cups corn kernels and place in a dry non-stick skillet. Cook on high heat for 2 to 3 minutes or until the kernels are lightly browned.

4 cobs corn	**CORIANDER CHILI MAYONNAISE**
1 carrot, peeled and slivered	½ cup mayonnaise
2 small zucchini, slivered	1½ tsp chili powder
1 red pepper, seeded and cut in strips	2 cloves garlic, finely chopped
1 green pepper, seeded and cut in strips	¼ cup lime juice
1 red onion, thinly sliced	2 tbsp chopped fresh coriander
3 cups shredded grilled	¼ tsp hot red pepper flakes
or cooked chicken	Salt and freshly ground pepper to taste

Place corn cobs on grill or under broiler and grill, turning occasionally, for 5 minutes. Scrape kernels off cobs.

Combine corn, carrot, zucchini, peppers, red onion and chicken in large bowl.

Combine mayonnaise, chili powder, garlic, lime juice, coriander, hot pepper flakes, salt and pepper in small bowl.

Stir together dressing and salad. Pile salad onto serving platter.

FRESH CORIANDER

Cilantro is the Spanish word for fresh coriander, but now that Asian cooking is superseding Mexican and Southwestern, the term coriander is used much more frequently. Both refer to the same flowery green herb.

THAI BEEF SALAD

SERVES 4

Thai fish sauce is an essential ingredient in Thai cooking. It is made from brined fish and is pungently salty, but it mellows when it is mixed with other ingredients.

Use leftover steak or storebought roast beef for this cool, herbal salad. This recipe can be made a day ahead and refrigerated until serving. If you want to serve this Thai style, wrap the salad and noodles in lettuce leaves and eat as finger food.

8 oz rice noodles	8 oz cooked steak or roast beef
1/2 cup lemon juice	1/2 cup chopped fresh coriander
1 tsp grated lemon rind	1 cup chopped fresh mint
3 tbsp Thai fish sauce or soy sauce	1 small red onion, thinly sliced
2 tsp granulated sugar	1/4 cup finely chopped almonds, toasted
1 tsp Asian chili sauce or to taste	2 cups bean sprouts
2 tbsp vegetable oil	1 head leaf lettuce

Place noodles in bowl, cover with hot water and soak for 30 minutes.

Bring pot of water to boil. Add noodles and cook for 1 minute. Drain well.

Combine lemon juice and rind, fish sauce, sugar, chili sauce and oil in small bowl.

Cut beef into slivers and place in separate bowl. Stir in coriander, mint, red onion, almonds and bean sprouts.

Pour half of dressing over vegetables and half of dressing over noodles. Pile meat mixture on lettuce-lined platter and surround with noodles.

TOASTING NUTS

Toasting nuts makes them more flavorful. Spread the shelled nuts on a baking sheet and bake at 350 F for 8 to 10 minutes or until golden. If you are toasting hazelnuts, rub them in a cloth after baking to remove the skins.

INSTANT MEDITERRANEAN TUNA SALAD

SERVES 4

I call this my instant salad because everything you need is already in the store cupboard or refrigerator. You can use store-bought grilled peppers or, for a time-consuming gourmet delight, make it with fresh grilled tuna, home-cooked white beans and your own grilled peppers. Make ahead of time and serve on mixed peppery greens such as arugula, frisee, radicchio and curly endive, if desired.

1 6½-oz (184 g) can solid white tuna, drained	**TARRAGON MAYONNAISE**
1 19-oz (540 mL) can white beans, drained and rinsed	½ cup mayonnaise
	2 tbsp sour cream
	1 tsp Worcestershire sauce
1 red pepper, grilled and chopped	2 tbsp lemon juice
1 cup chopped pitted olives	2 tbsp chopped fresh tarragon
1 cup chopped red onion	or 2 tsp dried
. . . . .	2 anchovies, chopped

Combine tuna, beans, red pepper, olives and onion in large bowl.

Whisk together mayonnaise, sour cream, Worcestershire, lemon juice, tarragon and anchovies

Toss half of dressing with tuna. Serve remaining dressing separately.

PEPPERED TUNA NIÇOISE SALAD

SERVES 6

An updated version of Niçoise salad featuring a spicy, peppered tuna steak. This can be served as a filling first course or a light supper dish. Try salmon in place of tuna for a different flavor. Use good-quality black olives (not canned) such as Kalamata.

1 tsp Dijon mustard	8 oz green beans, trimmed
1 tbsp chopped fresh tarragon	2 tomatoes, cut in wedges
or 1 tsp dried	1 red onion, thinly sliced
3 tbsp wine vinegar	2 hard-boiled eggs, cut in wedges
1/2 cup olive oil	1 cup black olives, pitted
Salt and freshly ground pepper to taste	1 tbsp olive oil
12 mini potatoes	1 lb tuna
1 head red leaf lettuce	1 tbsp cracked peppercorns (page 56)

Whisk together mustard, tarragon and wine vinegar. Slowly whisk in oil. Season with salt and pepper and reserve dressing.

Boil potatoes in pot of salted water until crisp-tender, about 8 minutes. Drain and toss with 2 tbsp dressing.

Add beans to pot of boiling water and cook for 3 minutes. Refresh under cold water.

Line large platter with lettuce. Arrange potatoes, green beans, tomatoes, red onion, hard-boiled eggs and olives in sections on platter.

Heat baking sheet under broiler for 5 minutes. Brush oil on tuna and coat with peppercorns. Place on heated baking sheet and broil for 5 to 6 minutes without turning. The tuna should be medium-rare in the middle.

Slice tuna into thin slices and place on platter. Drizzle salad with remaining dressing.

ASIAN SALMON SALAD WITH RICE NOODLES

SERVES 4

A tasty summer salad with Oriental flavors.

1 lb salmon fillet	3 cups bean sprouts
1 tbsp soy sauce	• • • • •
pinch granulated sugar	2 tbsp lemon juice
1 tbsp grated ginger	1 tbsp Thai fish sauce
4 oz thin rice noodles	1 tsp granulated sugar
1 tbsp vegetable oil	1/2 tsp Asian chili sauce
1 red onion, thinly sliced	1 tbsp vegetable oil
1 cup slivered fresh mint	• • • • •

Remove skin from salmon and cut fish into thin strips.

Combine soy sauce, sugar and ginger. Pour over salmon and marinate for 30 minutes.

Place rice noodles in bowl. Cover with hot water and let soak for 30 minutes.

Bring pot of water to boil. Boil noodles until softened, about 1 minute. Drain well and cool under cold running water.

Add oil to wok or non-stick skillet on high heat. Add salmon and sauté until pink but still slightly rare, about 1 minute. Remove from heat.

Combine noodles, salmon, onion, mint and bean sprouts in large bowl.

Combine lemon juice, fish sauce, sugar, chili sauce and vegetable oil in small bowl. Toss salad with dressing.

RICE NOODLES

Rice noodles come in different thicknesses and are available fresh or dried at supermarkets and Asian grocery stores. Most recipes call for dried noodles, because they are easier to find. They must be soaked in hot water for 30 minutes before cooking.

Broad rice noodles are used in Pad Thai dishes; thin noodles are usually used in salads and stir-fries.

CHAPTER 4

Fish and Seafood

We only eat to live when we don't understand how to live to eat.
—George Elwanger

SALMON WITH BLACK PEPPER AND GINGER

SERVES 4

Serve this salmon with cooked green lentils or rice.

4 6-oz salmon fillets
1 tbsp cracked peppercorns
1 tbsp grated ginger
Salt to taste

Cover fillets with peppercorns, ginger and salt.

Heat non-stick skillet on high heat. Place fillets skin side down and sear for 1 minute.

Cover skillet and reduce heat to low. Steam for 6 to 10 minutes or until white juices just begin to rise up.

Remove skin before serving, if desired.

CRACKING PEPPERCORNS

Place whole black peppercorns in a plastic bag and bang the bag with the bottom of a heavy pot until the peppercorns are in coarse pieces.

MEDITERRANEAN SALMON

SERVES 4

Poaching fish in a prepared sauce gives enormous flavor to the fish. You could also use this method to cook the fish in a curry sauce, a Mexican chili sauce or an Italian tomato sauce.

2 tbsp olive oil	2 cups pureed tomatoes
3 cloves garlic, sliced	1 tsp chopped fresh thyme or ¼ tsp dried
½ cup finely chopped onion	½ cup pitted black olives
¼ cup finely chopped carrot	4 6-oz salmon fillets, skin removed
1 cup white wine	Salt and freshly ground pepper to taste

Heat olive oil in skillet on medium-low heat. Add garlic, onion and carrot and sauté slowly until softened, about 6 to 8 minutes. Raise heat to medium, add wine and reduce by half, about 5 minutes.

Add tomatoes and thyme and cook for 10 minutes or until sauce has thickened. Add olives.

Place salmon on top of sauce. Cover pan and steam fish for 6 to 10 minutes or until just pink in center.

SALMON

The most popular way to buy salmon today is in fillets. For the most flavor, cook salmon with the skin on and then remove it before serving. Salmon comes from both the Atlantic and Pacific but most of it is farmed. Atlantic salmon is fattier than Pacific, and has a less delicate texture and more intense flavor.

CRISPY-SKINNED SALMON WITH CONFIT SPICES

SERVES 4

This is a wonderful method for cooking salmon and other full-flavored oily fish with skin, such as sea bass or grouper. The combination of frying and steaming makes the flesh moist and the taste exceptional. Serve with French fries and Caramelized Cabbage (page 147).

2 tbsp olive oil	1 tsp chopped garlic
4 6-oz salmon fillets, with skin	pinch dried thyme
1 tbsp coarsely ground pepper	pinch dried rosemary
1 tsp coarse salt	1 bay leaf, crumbled

Brush 1 tbsp oil on salmon fillets.

Combine pepper, salt, garlic, thyme, rosemary and bay leaf. Sprinkle on salmon. Marinate for 2 hours at room temperature or up to 4 hours in the refrigerator.

Heat remaining 1 tbsp oil in non-stick skillet on medium heat. Add salmon skin side down. Cover and cook for 6 to 8 minutes or until salmon is cooked but still slightly pink in center.

Remove skin from salmon. Place salmon on serving dish. Cut crisp skin into slivers and sprinkle over salmon.

CONFIT

Confit is a French preparation originally used to preserve geese, duck and pork in the days before refrigeration. The meat is seasoned with coarse salt, pepper and herbs and left to brine for 24 hours. It is then cooked very slowly in goose fat or lard until it practically falls off the bone. Stored in a ceramic crock and covered with the fat, it can keep for a few months.

ROASTED WHOLE FISH WITH SICILIAN SAUCE

SERVES 4

A traditional Sicilian sauce gives lots of flavor to the mild snapper. Use any small whole fish or firm fillets such as tuna or swordfish. I find that fish stays moister if you cook it whole, but remove the head if it bothers you.

2 tbsp chopped fresh oregano or 2 tsp dried	¾ cup olive oil
2 cloves garlic, chopped	2 2-lb whole red snappers
3 tbsp lemon juice	Salt and pepper to taste
	4 bay leaves

Preheat oven to 450 F.

Combine oregano and garlic in food processor or by hand with a mortar and pestle until paste-like. Add lemon juice and slowly whisk in ½ cup olive oil. Reserve sauce.

Make 2 slashes in each fish down to the bone. Rub with remaining ¼ cup olive oil, salt and pepper. Place 2 bay leaves in each cavity. Place in baking dish.

Roast fish for about 15 minutes or until white juices start to appear. Place on serving platter. Remove top fillets of fish and serve with sauce. Remove bones and serve bottom fillets with more sauce.

ROASTED SEA BASS WITH RED WINE SAUCE

SERVES 4

A superb dish for a dinner party. Serve with roasted potatoes and green beans sautéed with a touch of garlic.

1 tbsp Dijon mustard	½ cup orange juice
1 tbsp chopped fresh rosemary	1 tsp granulated sugar
or 1 tsp dried	1 tbsp balsamic vinegar
2 tbsp soy sauce	½ cup red wine
2 tbsp olive oil	2 tbsp butter
1½ lb sea bass, in one piece	• • • • •

Preheat oven to 450 F.

Combine mustard, rosemary, soy sauce and oil. Place sea bass in baking dish and brush with mustard mixture.

Bake fish for about 10 minutes per inch of thickness. It is ready when white juices rise to top and fish feels firm to the touch.

Heat orange juice, sugar, vinegar and red wine in skillet on high heat. Reduce until ¼ cup remains. Pour in any fish juices, bring to boil, remove from heat and beat in butter.

Slice fish into serving pieces and coat with sauce.

ROASTING FISH

To achieve the perfect roasted fish, roast at 450 F for 10 minutes per inch of thickness. Measure the fish vertically at its thickest point for the most accurate timing.

SAUTÉED SEA BASS WITH GARLIC, ROSEMARY AND WINE

SERVES 4

Use any thick-fleshed white fish for this dish. Grouper, monkfish, halibut and orange roughy all work well but watch the timing to make sure they are just cooked through.

4 6-oz sea bass fillets, skin removed	3 tbsp olive oil
1 tsp grated ginger	2 bay leaves
Salt and freshly ground pepper to taste	1 cup white wine
8 cloves garlic, thinly sliced	1 to 2 tsp balsamic vinegar
1 tbsp chopped fresh rosemary	2 tbsp hot water
or 1 tsp dried	2 tbsp butter, cold, cut in small pieces

Season fish with ginger, salt and pepper.

Combine garlic and rosemary.

Heat olive oil in skillet on medium heat. Add sea bass, flesh side down, and cook for about 2 minutes or until browned. Turn and cook skin side for 2 minutes.

Add garlic-rosemary mixture and bay leaves to skillet. Sauté for 1 minute.

Add wine, reduce heat to medium-low, cover and cook for 7 to 10 minutes or until white juices rise and fish is cooked. Remove fish, bring sauce to boil and simmer for 1 minute.

Reduce heat to medium-low. Add balsamic vinegar to skillet. Beat in hot water and cold butter and cook for 1 minute. Sauce should thicken. Pour sauce over fish.

SEA BASS

Chilean sea bass fillets are the new darling on the fish scene. Thick and mild flavored with no bones, sea bass cooks like a dream. The texture is buttery and it is difficult to overcook it. The other type of sea bass is striped bass. Prepare it as you would red snapper.

ROASTED FISH WITH POTATOES AND ARTICHOKES

SERVES 4

A superb all-in-one dinner party dish with Mediterranean flavors. Buy roasted artichokes if you can find them; they have much more taste than canned or marinated.

3 Yukon Gold or baking potatoes, peeled and sliced

1/4 cup olive oil

2 tsp chopped garlic

3 bay leaves

12 black olives, pitted

1/4 cup white wine

4 roasted or canned artichokes, quartered

4 6-oz pieces sea bass, snapper or other white fish

Salt and freshly ground pepper to taste

Preheat oven to 450 F.

Boil potatoes in water to cover until crisp-tender, about 5 to 7 minutes. Drain and place in bowl. Toss with olive oil, garlic, bay leaves, olives, wine and artichokes. Place in baking dish.

Season fish with salt and pepper. Place on top of potatoes.

Bake for 15 to 20 minutes or until potatoes are crusty and fish is cooked.

BAKED SNAPPER PROVENÇAL

SERVES 4

Serve this easy dish with rice, couscous or noodles. Add a salad and good bread to mop up the juices. Substitute striped bass, tilapia or sole for the snapper, if preferred.

2 tbsp olive oil	1 cup drained and chopped canned tomatoes
1 small onion, chopped	1 tbsp chopped fresh basil or 1 tsp dried
2 cloves garlic, chopped	½ tsp fennel seeds, optional
¼ cup white wine	1½ lb red snapper fillets

Preheat oven to 375 F.

Heat oil in skillet on high heat. Add onion and garlic. Sauté for 2 minutes or until slightly softened.

Add wine, tomatoes, basil and fennel to skillet. Bring to boil for 1 minute, then reduce heat and simmer for 5 minutes or until slightly thickened.

Place fish in buttered baking dish that will hold it in one layer. Top with sauce.

Bake for 10 minutes or until fish is opaque and white juices start to rise. Serve from baking dish.

BUYING FISH

You need a good fishmonger to tell you when fish comes in fresh and to advise you on what fish to select for a particular recipe. If you are buying whole fish, the eyes should be clear, not cloudy. Fresh fish should never have an odor and, when the skin is pressed, it should spring right back. Fish fillets should be translucent, with a slight sheen.

STORING FISH

Store fish in the refrigerator in a dish covered with a paper towel or cloth. (Leaving it wrapped in plastic will cause it to deteriorate quickly.) If you are cooking frozen fish, defrost it overnight in the refrigerator.

THAI GROUPER

SERVES 4

Thai green curry paste is sold in cans in Asian grocery stores and some supermarkets. If it is unavailable, call the dish Indian Grouper and make it using madras or vindaloo curry paste.

1 tbsp vegetable oil	1 cup coconut milk
3 cloves garlic, chopped	2 tbsp lime juice
4 shallots, chopped	2 tbsp chopped fresh coriander or mint
1 tsp green Thai curry paste	4 6-oz grouper fillets

Heat oil in non-stick skillet on medium heat. Add garlic and shallots and sauté for 2 minutes. Add Thai curry paste and cook for 1 minute.

Add coconut milk and lime juice. Bring to boil and simmer for 5 minutes or until thickened. Stir in coriander.

Place grouper on top of sauce. Cover and cook for 6 to 8 minutes or until fish is just opaque in center.

COCONUT MILK

Coconut milk comes in cans from Thailand and China. There is a thin liquid and a thicker paste in each can; shake well before opening. Coconut milk does not keep well, so freeze any leftovers.

VINEYARD CHICKEN (PAGE 86)

HERBED VEAL CHOPS (PAGE 108)

FRIED FISH

SERVES 3 TO 4

This is a generic recipe for frying fish. You can use tilapia, catfish, sole, flounder, red snapper, cod or haddock. Using cornmeal or cracker crumbs will add crunch, or you can add ¼ cup finely chopped pecans, hazelnuts or almonds to the flour for a nutty texture and taste. Serve with lemon slices.

¼ cup all-purpose flour	1 lb fish fillets (about 4)
Salt and freshly ground pepper to taste	1 cup dry breadcrumbs, cornmeal
1 egg	or cracker crumbs
5 tbsp vegetable oil	. . . . .

Combine flour, salt and pepper in shallow dish.

Beat egg with 1 tbsp oil in separate shallow dish.

Dip fish pieces into flour. Then dip in egg mixture. Coat fish with breadcrumbs.

Heat remaining 4 tbsp oil in large skillet on medium heat. Add fish but do not crowd. Fry until golden-brown. Turn and fry on second side, about 5 minutes total cooking time.

BROILED FISH STEAKS WITH TWO-TOMATO SALSA

SERVES 4

A generic recipe for broiling fish steaks. Use fish such as halibut, salmon or grouper (center-cut steaks are tastier than those from the tail end).

4 8-oz fish steaks	1/2 cup diced ripe tomatoes
1 tsp finely chopped garlic	1/4 cup chopped fresh mint or basil
2 tbsp olive oil	2 tbsp chopped green onions
pinch cayenne	2 tbsp balsamic vinegar
1 tbsp balsamic vinegar	1 tbsp olive oil
1/2 cup chopped sun-dried tomatoes	Salt and freshly ground pepper to taste

Place steaks in large flat dish. In small bowl, combine garlic, oil, cayenne and vinegar. Pour over fish and turn to coat both sides. Cover and marinate for at least 30 minutes or refrigerate for up to 4 hours.

Pour hot water over sun-dried tomatoes and let sit for 10 minutes. Drain well.

Combine dried and fresh tomatoes, mint, green onions, vinegar and oil. Stir together until blended. Add salt and pepper and reserve salsa.

Place baking sheet under preheated broiler for 5 minutes. Remove from broiler and place fish on it. Fish will sizzle. Broil for about 5 to 8 minutes or until white juices appear. Do not turn fish. To serve, spoon salsa over each steak.

BROILING FISH

The secret to perfect broiled fish is to use a heavy ovenproof skillet or baking sheet that you preheat on top of the stove or in the oven. Oil the fish lightly, place on the preheated surface, then place under the broiler. The fish cooks on both the top and bottom without requiring turning.

SWORDFISH STEAKS WITH RED PEPPER ROUILLE

SERVES 4

Swordfish is a firm, oily, flavorful fish. Brush it with oil during cooking and serve slightly pink. For a quick first course before the swordfish, buy tapenade, spread it on toasts and serve with an arugula, radicchio and Belgian endive salad.

A rouille is a pungent Mediterranean mixture of chilies, garlic and olive oil. Adding red peppers and yogurt softens this version. This low-fat dip is also excellent with chicken wings, veggies and breadsticks. You can also add ½ cup sun-dried tomatoes to the peppers.

RED PEPPER ROUILLE	
2 red peppers	1 tsp cracked coriander seeds
1 jalapeño pepper	1 tsp cracked peppercorns (page 56)
2 cloves garlic, chopped	1 tbsp lemon juice
½ cup plain yogurt	¼ cup olive oil
1 tbsp olive oil	4 8-oz swordfish steaks, about
	1 inch thick

Cut red peppers and jalapeño in half and remove seeds. Place cut side down on baking sheet and broil for 3 to 5 minutes or until skin is black and blistered. Let peppers cool slightly, then peel.

Combine peppers in food processor or blender with garlic, yogurt and oil. Puree until smooth. Taste for seasoning, adding salt if needed. Reserve.

Combine coriander, pepper, lemon juice and olive oil. Brush on fish steaks and marinate for 30 minutes.

Place baking sheet under preheated broiler for 5 minutes. Place fish on baking sheet. Broil for 5 to 8 minutes or until fish is still slightly pink in center. Do not turn fish. Serve topped with rouille.

SEARED TUNA WITH JAPANESE NOODLES

SERVES 4

A delightful, easy main course. The tuna can also be grilled on the barbecue. Cook it rare for the best flavor. For an attractive presentation, decorate the plate with the wasabi sauce piped from a squeeze bottle.

2 tsp wasabi powder or paste

1/2 cup mayonnaise

3 tbsp whipping cream

8 oz udon noodles (page 74)

2 tbsp vegetable oil

6 shiitake mushrooms, stemmed and thinly sliced

1 tbsp grated ginger

1 tbsp mirin or sherry

1 tsp sesame oil

2 tbsp soy sauce

1 tbsp rice vinegar

3 green onions, slivered

4 8-oz tuna steaks, about 1 inch thick

Salt and freshly ground pepper to taste

• • • • •

Combine wasabi, mayonnaise and whipping cream. Thin with a little water if too thick.

Cook noodles in boiling water until *al dente*. Drain well.

Heat 1 tbsp oil in large skillet on medium-high heat. Add mushrooms and ginger and sauté until softened, about 1 minute.

Stir in mirin, sesame oil, soy sauce, vinegar and green onions. Stir in noodles and keep warm.

Heat remaining 1 tbsp oil in skillet on medium-high heat. Season tuna with salt and pepper. Sear tuna for 2 minutes per side (or longer if desired).

Divide noodle mixture among serving plates. Thinly slice tuna and place on top. Spoon wasabi mayonnaise on to tuna.

MIRIN

Mirin is a very sweet Japanese cooking wine available in grocery stores. If it is unavailable, add a small amount of sugar to the dish.

WASABI

Wasabi is a Japanese horseradish that comes in paste form in a tube or as a powder that you mix with water. It has a distinctive fragrance and flavor, but you can combine equal amounts of hot mustard and horseradish as a substitute.

JERK TUNA

SERVES 4

Lethally hot Scotch bonnet peppers are usually used in Caribbean cooking. If you can't find them, use jalapeños. This recipe works equally well with swordfish, grouper, halibut or chicken. Serve it with Coconut Rice and Peas (page 135).

1 bunch green onions, chopped	2 bay leaves, crumbled
3 cloves garlic, chopped	1 Scotch bonnet pepper, seeded and
Salt to taste	chopped, or to taste
2 tsp dried thyme	2 tbsp lime juice or cider vinegar
2 tsp ground allspice	3 tbsp vegetable oil
¼ tsp cinnamon	4 8-oz tuna steaks, about 1 inch thick
½ tsp grated nutmeg	• • • • •

Combine green onions, garlic, salt, thyme, allspice, cinnamon, bay leaves, hot pepper and lime juice in food processor. With machine on, add oil through feeder tube until a thick paste forms.

Rub paste into tuna and marinate for 1 hour at room temperature.

Grill or broil tuna for 2 to 3 minutes per side or until tuna is cooked but still pink in center.

SPICY FISH WITH ASIAN ONIONS

SERVES 4

Use a firm-fleshed fish such as swordfish, sea bass, marlin, salmon or mahi mahi. If the fish has a skin, cook it flesh side down first, then turn and cook skin side down. Serve with rice.

2 tbsp soy sauce	Salt to taste
1 tbsp grated ginger	3 tsp vegetable oil
1 tsp cracked peppercorns (page 56)	1 Spanish onion, thinly sliced
pinch cayenne, optional	1 tbsp slivered garlic
4 6-oz fish fillets	1 tbsp rice vinegar or cider vinegar

Combine 1 tbsp soy sauce, ginger, pepper and cayenne. Brush on fish and marinate for 30 minutes to 2 hours. Salt fish lightly.

Heat 2 tsp oil in skillet on high heat. Add onion and sauté for 1 minute or until slightly softened. Add garlic and sauté for 1 minute longer. Reduce heat to medium-low, add remaining 1 tbsp soy sauce and vinegar and cook until onions are soft and turning golden, about 5 to 8 minutes.

Heat non-stick skillet on medium-high heat. Add remaining 1 tsp oil. Place fish in pan flesh side down and fry for 3 minutes or until golden. Turn and fry for 2 to 3 minutes longer or until just cooked.

Place fish on serving dishes and top with onions.

COOKING FISH

Thin-fleshed fish such as tilapia, catfish and sole are best sautéed in a skillet either with a coating or with a quick dusting of flour. Poaching in liquid is another low-calorie option.

Thicker-fleshed fish such as halibut, Chilean sea bass, salmon, grouper or mahi mahi can be sautéed, but are best roasted, grilled, steamed or cooked with a sauce.

Fish such as mackerel, kingfish and herring are best fried or grilled because of their rich flavor and their tendency to be oily.

GRILLED SHRIMP WITH SANTA FE SALSA

SERVES 4

A good first course before beef or lamb. Try passing the shrimp as a cold hors d'oeuvre before dinner, too.

SANTA FE SALSA

2 red peppers, halved and seeded	½ cup olive oil
2 jalapeño peppers, halved and seeded	Grated rind and juice of 1 lemon
½ cup chopped fresh coriander	Salt to taste
1 shallot, chopped	2 tsp dried basil
1 clove garlic, chopped	¼ cup chopped parsley
¼ cup pine nuts, toasted (page 51)	2 cloves garlic, finely chopped
Grated rind and juice of 1 lime	1 tsp cayenne
¼ cup olive oil	1 tbsp chili powder
Salt and freshly ground pepper to taste	16 large shrimp, shelled

Place red and jalapeño peppers on baking sheet skin side up and broil for 5 minutes or until skin is black and blistered. Remove from heat and cool, then peel.

Combine peppers, coriander, shallot, garlic, pine nuts, lime rind and juice in food processor or blender. Process just until chopped.

Pour olive oil gradually through feed tube and process until combined but not pureed. Season with salt and pepper.

Combine olive oil, lemon rind and juice, salt, basil, parsley, garlic, cayenne and chili powder in large bowl. Add shrimp and marinate for 2 hours at room temperature or overnight in refrigerator.

Grill or broil shrimp on high heat, turning once, for 3 to 5 minutes or until pink and slightly curled.

Spoon sauce over shrimp or serve as a dip.

STIR-FRIED SHRIMP AND ASPARAGUS

SERVES 4

A quick spicy stir-fry for asparagus season. Substitute sugar snaps or snow peas, if desired. Serve with rice or noodles.

2 tbsp vegetable oil	1 lb shrimp, shelled
1 tbsp grated ginger	2 tbsp soy sauce
1 tsp chopped garlic	2 tbsp oyster sauce
1/2 tsp Asian chili sauce	1/4 cup chicken stock
8 oz thin asparagus, trimmed and cut in 2-inch lengths	• • • • •

Heat oil in wok or skillet on high heat. Add ginger, garlic and chili sauce. Stir-fry for 30 seconds. Add asparagus and stir-fry for 1 minute.

Add shrimp and cook until pink, about 2 to 3 minutes. Add soy sauce, oyster sauce and stock. Bring to boil and serve immediately.

FLASH-FRIED SQUID

SERVES 4 AS AN APPETIZER; 2 AS A MAIN COURSE

A combination of flour and cornstarch gives you a crisper batter than flour alone. Serve the squid with Spiced Sauce.

1 lb squid	2 tbsp cornstarch
1 tbsp soy sauce	¼ cup all-purpose flour
1 tbsp coarsely ground pepper	Salt to taste
1 tbsp finely chopped garlic	Vegetable oil for frying

Rinse squid and cut into ½-inch rings. Season with soy sauce.

Combine pepper, garlic, cornstarch, flour and salt. Toss squid with flour mixture.

Heat oil in wok or deep-fryer on medium-high heat until a bread cube turns brown in 15 seconds. Add squid and cook for 1 minute or until golden. Remove immediately from oil and drain on paper towels.

SPICED SAUCE

Combine ¼ cup mayonnaise, ½ tsp Asian chili sauce and 1 tbsp lime juice.

Makes about ¼ cup.

SPICY SCALLOPS WITH SOBA NOODLES

SERVES 4

If soba or buckwheat noodles are unavailable, use egg or rice noodles. If mirin is unavailable, add ½ tsp granulated sugar.

SPICY SESAME SAUCE
1 tbsp sesame oil
1 tbsp vegetable oil
1 tsp wasabi paste or powder
2 tbsp soy sauce
2 tbsp rice vinegar
2 tsp mirin
· · · · ·
8 oz soba noodles
1 tbsp vegetable oil

1 tbsp sesame oil
½ red pepper, diced
2 tbsp grated ginger
1 tsp Asian chili sauce
1 lb scallops
1 bunch spinach, washed, trimmed and sliced
4 green onions, chopped
1 tbsp sesame seeds, toasted (page 87)

Combine all sauce ingredients.

Cook noodles in large pot of boiling water until *al dente* (the time will vary depending on the type of noodle). Drain. Toss with 2 tbsp sauce.

Heat vegetable and sesame oils in large skillet on high heat. Add red pepper and sauté for 1 minute. Add ginger, chili sauce and scallops. Sauté for 3 minutes or until scallops are just opaque.

Add noodles and spinach and stir-fry until spinach is just wilted, about 2 minutes. Add green onions and remaining sauce. Toss together until hot and serve garnished with sesame seeds.

JAPANESE NOODLES

There are many different kinds of Japanese noodles. Thin and brownish-gray in color, *soba* noodles are made with buckwheat flour and water. Substitute *somen* (fine white vermicelli noodles) or *udon* (thick flour and water noodles), egg noodles or rice noodles.

Japanese noodles are available frozen, fresh or dried. To prepare them, follow the package instructions.

MOUCLADE

SERVES 4 AS AN APPETIZER; 2 AS A MAIN COURSE

A sensational, piquant soup-appetizer dish very popular on France's Brittany coast. Serve with French fries and a sharp green salad for a main course.

1 tbsp butter	1 cup white wine
1 small onion, chopped	2 lb mussels, cleaned
1 clove garlic, chopped	1 cup whipping cream
1 tsp curry powder	Salt and freshly ground pepper to taste
1/2 tsp fennel seeds, crushed, optional	2 tbsp chopped parsley

Heat butter in large pot on medium heat. Add onion, garlic, curry powder and fennel seeds. Sauté for 1 minute. Add wine and bring to boil. Stir in mussels (discard any that are open before cooking), cover and cook for 2 to 3 minutes or until mussels open, shaking pan occasionally.

Remove mussels (discard any that remain closed) and reduce liquid by half. Stir in cream and cook for 3 minutes or until slightly thickened. Add salt, pepper and parsley. Return mussels to pot, stir everything together and serve.

BETELNUT'S WOK-STEAMED MUSSELS

SERVES 2 TO 3

A betelnut is an exotic nut with a strange but addictive flavor. It grows throughout Southeast Asia. The restaurant Betelnut in San Francisco has many of the same qualities. The dishes come from all over Southeast Asia; this is their very simple but popular mussel dish.

1½ cups chicken stock

1 tsp chopped garlic

2 tsp sliced jalapeño pepper

or other hot pepper

10 Thai basil leaves or regular basil

4 Kaffir lime leaves (page 185)

or 1 tsp grated lime rind

½ cup diced tomatoes

1 tbsp Thai fish sauce

2 lb mussels, cleaned

Add stock, garlic, jalapeño, basil, lime leaves, tomatoes and fish sauce to large pot. Bring to boil.

Add mussels (discard any that are open before cooking), cover and cook for 2 to 3 minutes or until mussels open. Shake pan occasionally. Discard any unopened mussels.

Serve in large bowls.

CLEANING MUSSELS

Most mussels sold today are cultivated, or farmed. They need very little cleaning; just rinse them briefly and remove the hairy beards, if necessary. Wild mussels should be washed well and the beards removed. Strain the steaming liquid after cooking in case the mussels have expelled sand into it.

CHAPTER 5

Poultry

Spread the table and the quarrel will end.
—Hebrew proverb

CRISPY ROAST CHICKEN

SERVES 4

A trip to California provided this recipe for roast chicken with an extra-crispy skin and a shortened cooking time. Have the butcher butterfly the chicken for you by removing the backbone and breastbone so the chicken will lie flat.

3 tbsp chopped fresh tarragon	1 3¹/₂-lb chicken, butterflied
or 1 tbsp dried	¹/₄ cup balsamic or cider vinegar
Grated rind of 1 lemon	pinch granulated sugar
1 clove garlic, chopped	1 cup chicken stock
2 tbsp olive oil	2 tbsp butter
Salt and freshly ground pepper to taste	• • • • •

Preheat oven to 400 F.

Combine 2 tbsp tarragon, lemon rind, garlic, 1 tbsp olive oil, salt and pepper.

Lay chicken in roasting pan, skin side up. Rub tarragon mixture over chicken and marinate for 1 hour.

Turn chicken legs in toward breast. Heat remaining 1 tbsp oil in large skillet on medium heat. Brown chicken skin side down until a rich golden color, about 5 to 7 minutes. Press down on chicken with spatula as it cooks.

Turn chicken and brown on second side for 5 minutes.

Place chicken, skin side up, on rack in roasting pan or leave in ovenproof skillet. Roast, basting occasionally, for 30 to 40 minutes or until juices run clear. Remove chicken from oven and place on carving board.

Combine vinegar, sugar and remaining 1 tbsp tarragon in pot. Cook on medium-high heat for 2 minutes or until reduced to a glaze.

Pour in chicken stock and any accumulated chicken juices. Bring to boil and reduce until slightly thickened. Turn heat to low and whisk in butter.

Slice chicken through breast, then remove legs and thighs from each half. Serve with sauce.

SPATCHCOCK

The technical term for butterflied chicken is spatchcock, and it means to remove the backbone, breastbone and ribs from a chicken, then fold the legs in toward the breast. This provides protection for the breast during cooking.

CHICKEN WITH HERB SAUCE

SERVES 4

*A simple chicken dish with rich herbal tastes. Use any fresh herbs, but do not substitute dried.
I use parsley and coriander when nothing else is available.*

4 boneless, skinless single chicken breasts	2 tbsp chopped fresh basil
Salt and freshly ground pepper to taste	1/2 tsp grated lemon rind
2 tbsp butter	1/2 cup white wine
3 shallots, chopped, or 1/2 cup	1/2 cup apple juice
chopped red onion	1/4 cup whipping cream
1 tbsp chopped fresh mint	• • • • •

Season chicken breasts with salt and pepper.

Heat butter in skillet on medium heat. Add chicken breasts and cook for 3 to 4 minutes per side or until juices run clear. Remove from skillet.

Add shallots, mint, basil and lemon rind to skillet. Stir together until shallots soften, about 1 minute.

Pour in wine and apple juice, bring to boil and reduce until 2 tbsp remain.

Stir in whipping cream, bring to boil, return breasts and any chicken juices and simmer for 2 to 3 minutes or until breasts are heated through.

CHICKEN LEGS WITH MOLE SAUCE

SERVES 4

Mexican mole sauce, a heady mixture of chilies, spices, fruit and unsweetened chocolate, is often served with chicken or pork. The chocolate adds depth. This simplified version has lots of flavor but doesn't require the traditional lengthy preparation. For chili lovers, use a mixture of dried ancho and pasilla chilies; for the more timid, try New Mexican chilies for the mildest taste.

Chicken breasts on the bone or pork tenderloin can be substituted for the legs. The sauce may be made up to five days ahead of time. Serve with warm tortillas.

4 tbsp olive oil	1 tsp cumin seeds
4 chicken legs, separated into legs and thighs	1 large tomato, sliced
	1 tsp dried oregano
Salt and freshly ground pepper to taste	1/2 tsp cinnamon
6 dried ancho chilies	1/4 cup raisins
1 Spanish onion, sliced in thick rounds	2 cups chicken stock
4 cloves garlic, peeled	1 oz unsweetened chocolate,
2 tbsp sesame seeds	coarsely chopped
2 tbsp ground almonds	Chopped fresh coriander

Preheat oven to 400 F.

Heat 1 tbsp oil in large non-stick skillet on medium-high heat. Add chicken and cook for 3 minutes per side or until golden. Season with salt and pepper. Place in baking dish and bake for 20 minutes or until juices are clear.

Soak chilies, meanwhile, in boiling water for 30 minutes. Drain, stem and seed them. Place in food processor or blender.

Heat 2 tbsp oil in skillet on high heat. Add onion and garlic and sauté for 1 minute or until slightly browned.

Add sesame seeds, almonds and cumin to skillet and cook for 1 minute longer. Add tomato to skillet and cook for 2 minutes. Scrape mixture into food processor along with oregano, cinnamon, raisins, stock and chocolate. Process until smooth.

Add remaining 1 tbsp oil to skillet on medium-high heat. Place contents of food processor in skillet, bring to boil, reduce heat and simmer for 30 minutes. Season with salt and pepper.

Add chicken to mole sauce and cook until chicken is hot. Serve chicken and sauce sprinkled with coriander.

STUFFED CHICKEN BREASTS WITH MUSHROOM SAUCE

SERVES 4

A rich, interesting chicken dish perfect for a special dinner. You can omit the ham or replace it with cooked spinach, if desired.

4 boneless, skinless single chicken breasts	2 tbsp olive oil
4 slices prosciutto or smoked ham	4 oz mushrooms, sliced
4 slices mozzarella cheese	1 clove garlic, chopped
½ tsp dried basil	¼ cup white wine
Salt and freshly ground pepper to taste	½ cup whipping cream

Butterfly chicken breasts. Place a slice of ham and cheese on half of each breast. Sprinkle with basil, salt and pepper. Fold breasts over and press down to seal edges.

Heat oil in skillet on medium heat. Brown breasts for about 3 minutes per side. Remove from skillet.

Add mushrooms and garlic to skillet. Sauté until mushrooms are limp, about 3 minutes. Add wine and reduce down to 1 tbsp. Add cream and cook until slightly thickened.

Return chicken breasts and any juice to skillet and simmer together for 5 minutes.

BUTTERFLYING CHICKEN BREASTS

To butterfly a chicken breast, place your hand on top of the chicken and, with a sharp knife, slice horizontally through the center of the breast. Cut through to about ½ inch of the other side to create an area for stuffing.

CITRUS SPICED CHICKEN

SERVES 4

Chicken thighs on the bone will give the juiciest results, but boneless chicken breasts work, too (reduce the cooking time by a couple of minutes).

Grated rind and juice of 1 orange	2 lb chicken thighs or
Grated rind and juice of 1 lime	4 boneless chicken breasts
1 tbsp Dijon mustard	Salt and freshly ground pepper to taste
½ tsp hot red pepper flakes	2 tbsp vegetable oil
1 tsp ground cumin	1 tbsp honey
3 tbsp soy sauce	1 tbsp balsamic vinegar
4 tbsp chopped fresh coriander	2 tbsp butter

Combine rind and juice of orange and lime, mustard, hot pepper flakes, cumin, soy sauce and 2 tbsp coriander.

Place chicken in dish and pour half of marinade over chicken. Reserve remaining marinade. Marinate for 30 minutes to 4 hours, refrigerated.

Preheat oven to 375 F.

Remove chicken from marinade, draining well. Season with salt and pepper. Discard marinade.

Heat oil in skillet on medium-high heat. Fry chicken, skin side down, for 3 minutes. Turn and fry second side for 3 minutes.

Place chicken in baking dish and bake for 15 to 20 minutes or until juices run clear.

Combine remaining marinade, honey and balsamic vinegar in small saucepan. Bring to boil on high heat and simmer for 2 minutes. Reduce heat to low and whisk in butter. Stir in remaining 2 tbsp coriander. Pour sauce over chicken.

GRILLED LEMON CHICKEN

SERVES 4

Top-quality chicken breasts need not be covered up with marinades and spicy rubs that mask their flavor. This simple, quick grill with a final brush of flavorings gives the chicken a sublime taste. Ask your butcher to bone the breasts leaving the skin on, or you can use skinless breasts, which take only 10 minutes to cook but don't have quite as much flavor.
Serve the chicken with grilled lemon slices.

4 boneless single chicken breasts, with skin	¼ cup chopped fresh herbs (any combination of tarragon, thyme,
3 tbsp olive oil	chervil, basil, mint or coriander)
Salt and pepper to taste	¼ cup lemon juice

Brush chicken with 1 tbsp oil and season with salt and pepper.

Combine mixed herbs, lemon juice and remaining 2 tbsp olive oil. Brush on breasts.

Place chicken on grill, skin side down, and grill for about 7 minutes. Turn, brush skin with lemon mixture and grill for 5 minutes on second side. Turn once more, brush breasts with remaining lemon mixture and grill for 2 more minutes or until chicken juices run clear.

Grilled Lemon Slices

Cut lemon into slices ¼ inch thick and grill for 5 to 7 minutes per side.

CHICKEN WITH RED CHILI SAUCE

SERVES 4 TO 6

This outstanding, mildly flavored red chili sauce can be used with pork, fish or seafood. If you can find them, canned chipotle chilies in adobo (sauce) will add an intense, smoky flavor to this dish. The sauce can also be used in soups, sauces and salsas.

4 dried ancho chilies, seeded	1 tsp dried oregano
1 small onion, chopped	1 tsp honey
3 large cloves garlic, chopped	Salt to taste
1 plum tomato, chopped	1 tbsp olive oil
1 tsp chopped chipotle in adobo or to taste, optional	4 boneless single chicken breasts, with or without skin
1 tsp ground cumin	2 tbsp chopped fresh coriander

Cover chilies, onion, garlic, tomato and chipotle with water in small pot. Bring to boil and cook until chilies are soft, about 10 minutes. Drain, reserving 1 cup liquid.

Place chili mixture in food processor along with cumin, oregano and honey. Blend until smooth, adding enough soaking water to make a sauce. Season with salt.

Preheat oven to 350 F.

Heat oil in non-stick skillet on medium-high heat. Season breasts and brown for about 2 minutes on each side. Remove from skillet and reserve.

Add chili sauce to skillet and sauté for 2 minutes to intensify flavors.

Place sauce in baking dish and top with chicken. Bake for 15 to 25 minutes or until chicken juices run clear. Sprinkle with chopped fresh coriander.

CHICKEN IN THE POT THAI STYLE

SERVES 4

This Thai version of the French poule au pot *makes a light and fresh meal. Vary the vegetables to suit your own taste, making sure the harder ones go in at the beginning of cooking and the more delicate toward the end. For the stock, use one can of low-salt chicken broth plus water, or use good-quality stock cubes. Serve the soup as a starter and the chicken and vegetables with Spicy Lime Sauce as the main course.*

5 cups chicken stock	4 oz green beans, trimmed
4 slices ginger, smashed	2 zucchini, thickly sliced
4 Kaffir lime leaves (page 185) or	4 dried Chinese mushrooms, soaked
1 tsp grated lime rind	in hot water for 20 minutes, or 4 fresh
1 or 2 fresh chilies, left whole	shiitake mushrooms, stalks removed
2 stalks lemon grass	2 tbsp lime juice or to taste
1 3-lb chicken	2 tbsp Thai fish sauce or to taste
2 carrots, peeled and thickly sliced	Pepper to taste
3 leeks, trimmed, washed and halved	2 tbsp chopped fresh coriander
8 cloves garlic, peeled	• • • • •

Combine chicken stock, ginger, Kaffir lime leaves and chilies in large pot. Bring to boil and simmer for 5 minutes.

Discard all but 2 inches of lemon grass roots. Cut roots in half, smash and place in chicken cavity. Place chicken, breast side up, in stock. Add carrots and simmer for 15 minutes. Turn chicken, add leeks and garlic and simmer for 20 minutes.

Turn chicken breast side up again. Add green beans, zucchini and mushrooms. Simmer for 15 minutes or until chicken juices run clear. Remove chicken and vegetables and keep warm.

Season broth with lime juice, fish sauce and pepper. Discard ginger.

Skin and cut up chicken, discarding backbone. Place on platter with vegetables. Sprinkle with coriander.

SPICY LIME SAUCE

Whisk together 1 tsp chopped garlic, 1 tsp Asian chili sauce, 1 tbsp Thai fish sauce, ¼ cup water, 3 tbsp lime juice and 1 tbsp brown sugar. Stir in 2 tbsp grated carrot and 2 tbsp chopped mint.

Makes about ¾ cup.

VINEYARD CHICKEN

This method of cooking chicken produces a juicy, golden bird with a marvelous sauce.

1 3-lb chicken	½ cup sliced carrot
Salt and freshly ground pepper to taste	1 tbsp chopped fresh tarragon
1 tbsp butter	or 1 tsp dried
1 cup sliced onion	8 oz red grapes, halved and seeded

Preheat oven to 400 F.

Season chicken with salt and pepper.

Heat butter in ovenproof casserole on medium heat and brown breast side down until golden, about 3 minutes. Turn and brown on all sides, about 3 minutes per side. Remove chicken and drain off all but 1 tbsp fat.

Add onion and carrot to casserole and sauté for 1 minute. Add tarragon and grapes.

Return chicken to pan breast side up. Cover and bake for 55 minutes, basting occasionally.

Remove chicken from pan to carving board and cover with tea towel to keep warm. Skim fat from casserole.

Scrape contents of casserole into food processor. Process until smooth. Return to pan, bring to boil and simmer for 1 minute or until flavors are combined (if sauce is too thick, thin with a little stock or water). Season with salt and pepper.

Carve chicken and serve with sauce. Garnish with extra grapes.

SESAME CHICKEN WITH SUGAR SNAPS

SERVES 4

A quick Chinese-style stir-fry to serve with rice.

2 tbsp vegetable oil	8 oz sugar snap peas, trimmed
1 clove garlic, chopped	1 tbsp water
1 tbsp grated ginger	1 tbsp soy sauce
1 lb boneless, skinless	1 tsp sesame oil
chicken breasts, cubed	1 tbsp sesame seeds, toasted
1 onion, sliced	• • • • •

Heat oil in wok or skillet on high heat. Add garlic, ginger and chicken. Stir-fry for 1 minute.

Add onion and snap peas and stir-fry until onion is limp, about 2 minutes.

Add water and soy sauce. Toss everything together. Cook, stirring occasionally, until chicken is cooked through and snap peas are crisp-tender, about 5 minutes.

Stir in sesame oil and sesame seeds.

TOASTING SESAME SEEDS

Toasting sesame seeds gives them greater flavor. Place in a dry skillet on medium-high heat and stir until golden, about 2 minutes.

CHICKEN CHILI

SERVES 4

The secret to this recipe is the slow cooking of the onion and pepper mixture, which gives a strong, layered flavor to the chili. To serve, place bowls of sliced avocado, chopped red onions, grated cheese and sour cream on the table. Serve the chili with warm flour tortillas and let people select their own garnishes.

3 tbsp olive oil	2 tsp chili powder
4 boneless, skinless single chicken breasts, cut in 3/4-inch pieces	2 tsp ground cumin
	2 tsp dried ground coriander
1 large onion, cut in 1/2-inch chunks	1 cup chopped canned tomatoes
1/2 red pepper, cut in 1/2-inch chunks	1 cup chicken stock
1/2 green pepper, cut in 1/2-inch chunks	Lime juice to taste
3 cloves garlic, chopped	Salt to taste
1 jalapeño pepper, chopped	1/4 cup chopped fresh coriander

Heat 1 tbsp oil in skillet on medium-high heat. Add chicken and sauté until slightly browned, about 2 minutes. Remove from skillet.

Heat remaining 2 tbsp oil in skillet on medium-low heat. Add onion and peppers and sauté until onions are softened, about 12 minutes. Add garlic, jalapeño, chili powder, cumin and ground coriander and sauté for 1 minute.

Add tomatoes and chicken stock to skillet. Increase heat and bring to boil. Reduce heat and simmer for 15 to 20 minutes or until thickened.

Return chicken to skillet and simmer for 5 minutes or until chicken is cooked through. Season with lime juice and salt. Garnish with coriander.

CHICKEN TAGINE WITH GREEN OLIVES

SERVES 6

This dish may be served on its own or as part of a Moroccan meal with couscous, a fish dish and several salads. It is not hot, but it is intensely flavored. Remove the chicken skin for a lower-fat dish.

Preserved lemons are occasionally available in Middle Eastern stores. They are lemons that have been brined with salt and lemon juice and preserved for up to a year.

4 tbsp lemon juice	2 tsp ground cumin
6 cloves garlic, chopped	2 tsp paprika
Salt and freshly ground pepper to taste	1/2 tsp cinnamon
12 chicken thighs or	1/2 tsp saffron, crushed, optional
6 chicken breasts, halved	1/4 cup chopped parsley
2 tbsp olive oil	1/4 cup chopped fresh coriander
2 onions, thinly sliced	1/3 cup chicken stock or water
2 tsp dried ground ginger	1/2 cup green olives
1/2 tsp hot red pepper flakes or to taste	1/2 preserved lemon, slivered, optional

Combine 2 tbsp lemon juice, 1 tbsp chopped garlic, salt and pepper in large bowl. Add chicken and marinate for 15 minutes.

Heat oil in large skillet on medium-high heat. Add chicken and sauté for 3 minutes per side or until golden. Remove chicken from skillet and reserve.

Add onions to skillet and sauté for 3 minutes or until softened. Stir in remaining garlic and cook for 1 minute.

Add ginger, hot pepper flakes, cumin, paprika, cinnamon, saffron, parsley, coriander, remaining 2 tbsp lemon juice and stock to skillet. Bring to boil. Reduce heat to medium-low. Return chicken to pan, cover and simmer for 15 minutes.

Add olives and preserved lemon and cook for 5 minutes or until chicken is cooked through.

SOUTHWESTERN CHICKEN AND RICE

SERVES 4

I don't use a lot of rice because I think it should be a background ingredient, not a filler, but to extend this dish, you can increase the rice to 1½ cups and the stock to 3 cups. Serve with a Romaine lettuce, orange and onion salad.

4 chicken legs, divided into legs and thighs	1 jalapeño pepper, seeded and diced, or to taste
3 tsp chili powder	2 cloves garlic, chopped
Salt and pepper to taste	1 cup uncooked long-grain rice
2 tbsp olive oil	2 cups chicken stock or water
1 onion, chopped	Juice of 1 lime
1 red pepper, diced	¼ cup chopped fresh coriander or basil
1 green pepper, diced	

Season chicken with 1 tsp chili powder, salt and pepper.

Heat oil in large deep skillet on medium heat and brown chicken about 5 minutes per side or until golden-brown. Remove chicken from skillet.

Pour off all but 1 tbsp fat. Add onion, peppers, jalapeño and garlic to skillet. Sauté for 3 minutes or until peppers soften slightly.

Add remaining 2 tsp chili powder, rice, stock and lime juice. Stir together and bring to boil.

Reduce heat to simmer and return chicken to skillet, tucking it into rice. Cover and simmer for 25 to 30 minutes or until rice is tender and chicken is cooked through.

Sprinkle with coriander just before serving.

INDIAN CHICKEN AND RICE

Substitute 2 tbsp curry paste for chili powder and add 1 tbsp grated ginger along with garlic. Sprinkle with crisply fried onions and hard-boiled egg slices just before serving.

ITALIAN CHICKEN AND RICE

Omit chili powder and jalapeño and season with 1 tsp dried thyme and 1 tsp dried oregano. Substitute 1 cup chopped canned tomatoes for 1 cup chicken stock.

CHICKEN WITH CRISP SAGE LEAVES

SERVES 4

As sage still grows robustly when other herbs fade away, I make this favorite chicken recipe to use them up. The leaves become crunchy on frying and add texture to the dish.

4 boneless, skinless single chicken breasts

Salt and pepper to taste

2 tbsp olive oil

40 fresh sage leaves

¹/₂ cup white wine

2 tbsp balsamic vinegar

2 tbsp butter

· · · · ·

Preheat oven to 400 F.

Season chicken breasts with salt and pepper.

Heat oil in ovenproof skillet on medium-high heat. Add sage leaves and sauté for 1 minute or until beginning to crisp. Add chicken breasts and sear for 2 minutes per side.

Place skillet in oven and bake for 10 minutes or until breasts are cooked through. Remove breasts and sage leaves from skillet to 4 plates and keep warm.

Discard any fat in skillet and add wine and balsamic vinegar. Deglaze on medium-high heat, scraping up any little bits at bottom.

Remove skillet from heat and whisk in butter. Glaze breasts with sauce.

BUTTER

I always use unsalted butter in cooking. I prefer the taste and I like to add my own salt to recipes as needed. Unsalted butter has a lower percentage of water than salted butter, so it is better for baking and cooking, especially if you are adding it to sauces.

CHICKEN BURGERS

SERVES 4

Serve on sesame seed buns with lettuce, tomatoes and onions and top with Spiced Chutney. These burgers may also be grilled on a barbecue.

1½ lb ground chicken

4 green onions, chopped

2 tbsp grainy Dijon mustard

1 tbsp soy sauce

2 cloves garlic, chopped

1 tbsp chopped fresh rosemary or tarragon or 1 tsp dried

Salt and freshly ground pepper to taste

Combine chicken, green onions, mustard, soy sauce, garlic, rosemary, salt and pepper and mix together gently.

Form mixture into 4 patties about ¾ inch thick.

Heat non-stick skillet on medium heat and brush with oil. Cook patties for about 4 minutes per side or until juices run clear.

SPICED CHUTNEY

Combine equal amounts of Dijon mustard and chutney.

YOGURT CUCUMBER SAUCE

Combine 1 cup plain yogurt, 1 cup grated cucumber and 1 finely chopped clove garlic. Add lemon juice and salt to taste.

Makes about 2 cups.

STUFFED TURKEY BREAST

SERVES 6 TO 8

Easier than dealing with the whole bird, turkey breasts make an excellent main course at Christmas. Stuff the breast up to four hours ahead of time and refrigerate until one hour before baking.

1 4-lb boneless turkey breast	1 egg, lightly beaten
2 tbsp butter	2 tbsp Dijon mustard
1 onion, chopped	1 tbsp maple syrup
1 tsp dried marjoram	1 tbsp cider vinegar
1/2 tsp dried tarragon	2 tbsp butter, melted
1 apple, peeled and finely chopped	2 tbsp all-purpose flour
1 1/2 cups fresh breadcrumbs	3 cups chicken or turkey stock
1/4 cup orange juice	Salt and freshly ground pepper to taste
2 tsp orange rind	• • • • •

Preheat oven to 375 F.

Place turkey breast on sheet of waxed paper. Make pocket along the long side of breast, cutting through to within 1 inch of the other side.

Heat skillet on medium heat and add butter. Sauté onion, marjoram, tarragon and apple until slightly softened, about 3 minutes. Add breadcrumbs, orange juice and rind.

Transfer stuffing to bowl and stir in egg. If stuffing is dry, add a little water.

Place stuffing down center of turkey breast. Fold over breast so edges meet. Skewer or sew edges together. Tie breast in 3 or 4 places to hold it in an even shape.

Combine mustard, maple syrup and vinegar to make glaze.

Place turkey on rack in roasting pan and brush on glaze. Pour melted butter over top.

Bake for 60 to 75 minutes, basting occasionally with glaze and pan juices. When cooked, roast will feel firm to the touch and the juices will run clear. Let rest on carving board for 15 minutes before slicing.

Pour all but 2 tbsp fat from roasting pan. Stir in flour and cook on medium-heat until flour browns slightly. Add stock and any remaining glaze. Season with salt and pepper. Serve sauce over sliced turkey.

CORNISH HENS WITH HONEY LIME SAUCE

SERVES 4

Substitute bone-in chicken breasts, if desired. Serve with rice and stir-fried vegetables. For extra zest, serve with Spicy Lime Sauce (page 85).

4 Cornish hens	2 tbsp honey
¼ cup olive oil	2 tbsp lime juice
1 tsp grated lime rind	dash hot pepper sauce, optional
1 tbsp grated ginger	2 tbsp chopped fresh mint
2 tbsp soy sauce	• • • • •

Remove backbones from hens and cut each hen in half. Remove wing tips.

Combine oil, lime rind, ginger and soy sauce. Brush on hens and marinate for 1 hour.

Preheat oven to 400 F.

Combine honey, lime juice, hot pepper sauce and mint for glaze.

Remove hens from marinade and discard marinade. Place hens on rack in roasting pan skin side up. Brush with glaze. Bake for 35 to 40 minutes, brushing hens with more glaze every 10 minutes, until hens are golden and juices no longer run pink.

Garnish with mint sprigs.

PEKING DUCK ROLLS

SERVES 6 AS AN APPETIZER; 4 AS A MAIN COURSE

A streamlined version of Peking duck for those who love the taste but not the lengthy preparation time. Use chicken breasts if duck is unavailable (cook the chicken until it is no longer pink) or buy take-out Chinese barbecued pork or duck instead of using duck breasts.

2 tbsp soy sauce

1 tbsp honey

4 duck breasts

Pepper to taste

1 tbsp vegetable oil

8 small flour tortillas

½ cup hoisin sauce

½ English cucumber, peeled and
cut in thin strips

6 green onions, halved and
cut in 3-inch lengths

• • • • •

Combine soy sauce and honey.

Score duck skin in a cross-hatch pattern to help release the fat. Brush duck with soy sauce mixture. Season well with pepper. Marinate for 30 minutes.

Preheat oven to 400 F.

Heat oil in large ovenproof skillet on medium-high heat. Add duck breasts, skin side down, and cook for 2 minutes. Discard fat, flip duck breasts over and cook for 2 minutes.

Place skillet in oven and bake for 10 to 12 minutes or until breasts are still slightly pink and skin is crisp. Let duck rest on carving board for 5 minutes.

Place tortillas overlapping on baking sheet. Cover with foil and bake for 5 minutes or until heated through.

Slice duck into thin slices.

Spread hoisin on tortillas. Add slices of duck, cucumber and green onion. Roll up and cut in half. Alternatively, place all ingredients on a platter and let people help themselves.

DUCK

Duck is one of my favorite meals, but making roast duck is often a messy proposition, so I prefer to cut up the duck and use the legs and breasts in different recipes. Peking duck is fatty with lots of flavor. Muscovy ducks are much leaner but can be tough unless treated properly.

CRISPED DUCK LEGS WITH RED CABBAGE

SERVES 4

Serve with roasted potatoes for a fine winter meal, or omit the cabbage and serve over a salad of peppery greens for a summer supper.

4 duck legs	3 cloves garlic, thinly sliced
Salt and freshly ground pepper to taste	2 tbsp balsamic vinegar
3 tbsp olive oil	1 tsp granulated sugar
1 small red cabbage, thinly sliced	4 green onions, slivered

Remove excess fat from duck legs. Place legs skin side down and cut on both sides of thigh bone. Remove bones and discard. Season legs with salt and pepper.

Preheat oven to 450 F.

Heat 2 tbsp oil in large skillet on medium-high heat. Add duck legs, skin side down, and cook for 3 minutes. Turn and cook for 3 minutes. Discard any fat from skillet and place in oven. Bake legs for 15 minutes or until juices run clear.

Heat remaining 1 tbsp olive oil in skillet on medium heat. Add cabbage and garlic and cook for 10 minutes, stirring occasionally, until cabbage is crisp-tender. Stir in vinegar and sugar. Bring to boil and season with salt and pepper. Stir in green onions. Cook for 1 minute.

Place cabbage on serving plates and top with duck legs.

CHAPTER 6

Meat

The nearer the bone, the sweeter the meat.
—English proverb

ROASTED BEEF TENDERLOIN WITH PORT SAUCE

SERVES 6

A sensational, easy roast for entertaining. The sauce is slightly sweet to complement the richness of the beef.

1 3-lb beef tenderloin

Salt and freshly ground pepper to taste

1 tbsp chopped fresh rosemary
or 1 tsp dried

1 tbsp Dijon mustard

1 tbsp soy sauce

1 tbsp olive oil

1 cup Port or Madeira

1 cup beef or veal stock or

2 tbsp balsamic vinegar

2 tbsp butter

• • • • •

Preheat oven to 450 F.

Season beef with salt and pepper.

Combine rosemary, mustard, soy sauce and olive oil. Brush over meat and place on rack in roasting pan.

Roast meat for 30 to 45 minutes or until desired degree of doneness. Remove from pan and keep warm. Discard any fat from pan.

Add Port to pan and cook on stove over medium-high until reduced to 2 tbsp.

Add stock and vinegar to pan. Bring to boil and cook until reduced by half. Reduce heat to low and whisk in butter.

Slice roast into slices ¼ inch thick and serve with drizzle of sauce.

ROASTING BEEF TENDERLOIN

Beef tenderloin (also called beef filet) is cooked by thickness, not by weight. Measure the thickest part vertically and calculate 15 minutes to the inch for rare, 20 minutes to the inch for medium-rare, 25 minutes for medium.

POT AU FEU NINETIES STYLE

SERVES 4

Pot au feu is a long-cooking, elaborate French soup/stew that includes beef, chicken and vegetables. It usually takes a couple of days to prepare, but my version is quick, low-fat and very tempting.

The better the stock, the better the dish. Good beef or veal stock is often available at gourmet food shops. If you use canned broth, buy a couple of marrow bones and simmer them with onions, carrots and celery, the can of broth and 5 cups of water for 30 minutes.

Measure the tenderloin vertically at its thickest point to determine timing. Poach for 10 minutes to the inch for rare.

6 cups beef or chicken stock	1 cup turnip sticks, cut ¼ inch thick
1½ lb beef tenderloin, about 2 inches thick	2 zucchini, cut in ¼-inch sticks
8 shallots, peeled and cut in half	4 baby bok choy, cut in half
1 cup carrot sticks, cut ¼ inch thick	through the root, optional

Bring stock to simmer in pot large enough to hold beef and vegetables. Add beef, shallots, carrot and turnip. Simmer for 10 minutes.

Add zucchini and bok choy to pot and simmer for 10 minutes or until vegetables are crisp-tender and beef is cooked to desired degree of doneness.

Divide vegetables among 4 soup bowls. Slice meat thinly and add to bowls. Pour over enough broth to moisten.

POT AU FEU GARNISHES

Pot au feu is traditionally served with a variety of garnishes. My favorites are coarse salt, cornichons, Dijon mustard, freshly ground black pepper, horseradish mixed with whipped cream, and chopped basil in oil. Place each garnish in a small bowl and serve on the side.

HUNAN BEEF WITH ASPARAGUS

SERVES 3 TO 4

This is my recipe tester's favorite dish in the book. The meat is so succulent that two people have been known to devour the whole thing.

The word ketchup is purported to come from China or Indonesia, where ketjap manis is a form of sweet soy sauce. Use the traditional tomato type in this recipe.

2 tbsp soy sauce	1 tbsp oyster sauce
1 tbsp all-purpose flour	1 tsp granulated sugar
3 slices ginger, smashed	1/4 tsp Asian chili sauce or to taste
1 tbsp sherry	1/4 cup water
1 egg white	Vegetable oil for frying
12 oz New York sirloin steak, cut in 1-inch cubes	8 oz asparagus, trimmed and cut in 2-inch pieces
1 tbsp ketchup	3 green onions, slivered

Combine 1 tbsp soy sauce, flour, ginger, sherry and egg white in large bowl. Stir in meat. Marinate for 30 minutes.

Combine remaining 1 tbsp soy sauce, ketchup, oyster sauce, sugar, chili sauce and water.

Heat 2 inches oil in wok on high heat until very hot. Remove beef from marinade and fry in batches for about 30 seconds. Beef should be rare. Drain in strainer while finishing the rest of beef.

Drain all but 2 tbsp oil from wok. Add asparagus and stir-fry for 1 minute. Add beef and sauce. Bring to boil and spoon onto serving platter. Sprinkle with green onions.

ROASTED SIRLOIN STEAK WITH MUSHROOM SAUCE

SERVES 6

Use a mixture of shiitake and oyster mushrooms in the sauce.

1 3½ lb sirloin steak, about 2 inches thick	2 tbsp olive oil
1 tbsp Dijon mustard	Salt and pepper to taste
3 cloves garlic, chopped	3 tbsp butter
2 tbsp soy sauce	8 oz wild mushrooms, sliced
1 tsp Worcestershire sauce	1 tbsp balsamic vinegar
2 tbsp chopped fresh rosemary or 2 tsp dried	1 cup red wine
1 tsp paprika	1½ cups beef or chicken stock
	2 tbsp chopped parsley

• • • • •

Trim fat from steak. Combine mustard, garlic, soy sauce, Worcestershire sauce, rosemary, paprika and 1 tbsp oil. Brush over both sides of steak. Season with salt and pepper. Marinate for 4 hours or overnight in refrigerator.

Preheat oven to 450 F.

Heat remaining 1 tbsp oil in large ovenproof skillet on medium-high heat. Add steak and cook for 3 minutes on each side. Place skillet in oven and bake for 15 to 18 minutes for rare, or until desired degree of doneness. Place on carving board and let rest while making sauce.

Heat 2 tbsp butter in skillet on medium-high heat. Add mushrooms and sauté until limp. Add balsamic vinegar and wine and reduce until ¼ cup remains. Add stock and reduce by half.

Reduce heat and stir in remaining 1 tbsp butter. Stir in parsley. Slice steak thinly and top with mushroom sauce.

CARAMELIZED SWEET ONIONS

Serve this versatile onion mixture on top of steaks or burgers or spread it on toast and top with Gorgonzola for an appetizer.

Heat 2 tbsp olive oil in heavy skillet on low heat. Add 3 sliced sweet onions (e.g., Vidalia or Spanish) and sauté slowly for about 20 minutes or until tender and golden. Add balsamic vinegar and cook until liquid is reduced. Season with salt and pepper to taste.

Makes about 1½ cups.

BISTRO BEEF STEAK WITH RED ONION MUSTARD SAUCE

SERVES 4

Serve this steak with Bistro Frites (page 162). The flank steak is fried for a more traditional taste, but you could also broil or barbecue it. Flank steak becomes tough if cooked to medium; medium-rare is best. Always carve the steak against the grain for the best results.

1½ lb flank steak	2 tsp tomato paste
3 tbsp olive oil	2 tbsp Dijon mustard
1 tsp dried thyme	1 tsp dried tarragon
1 tbsp coarsely ground pepper	½ cup beef or chicken stock
1 cup chopped red onion	2 tbsp whipping cream
3 cloves garlic, sliced	Salt to taste

Rub flank steak with 1 tbsp olive oil. Sprinkle with thyme and pepper. Marinate for 1 hour.

Cut steak into 4 pieces against grain.

Heat 1 tbsp oil in skillet on medium-high heat. Add red onion and garlic and sauté until softened and slightly brown, about 3 minutes.

Reduce heat to low. Add tomato paste, mustard, tarragon, stock and cream. Simmer for 1 minute and remove from heat.

Heat remaining 1 tbsp oil in large skillet on high heat. Add steak pieces and cook for 3 to 4 minutes, pressing down occasionally. Season with salt, turn and cook for 2 to 3 minutes or until juices just begin to rise.

Remove steak from pan and let rest for 2 minutes. Carve each portion into thick slices against the grain. Serve topped with sauce.

CHILI CITY STYLE

SERVES 6

Chili is best when it is made with diced beef. This gives you more texture and flavor than ground meat, although you can substitute ground meat if desired. Serve the chili with condiments such as sour cream, chopped onion, grated cheese and chopped peppers.

2 tbsp vegetable oil	1 tbsp dried ground coriander
2 lb stewing beef, diced	1 tsp dried oregano
Salt and freshly ground pepper to taste	1/4 tsp cayenne
1 large onion, chopped	1 cup beef stock
4 cloves garlic, finely chopped	2 cups canned tomatoes, pureed
3 tbsp chili powder	1 19-oz (540 mL) can
1 tbsp ground cumin	kidney beans, drained

Heat oil in large pot on high heat. Add beef and brown, about 4 minutes. Remove from pan. Season with salt and pepper.

Reduce heat to medium and add onion. Cook for 3 minutes or until softened. Add garlic and cook for 30 seconds.

Return meat to pot and stir together with onions. Stir in chili powder, cumin, coriander, oregano and cayenne. Cook for 1 minute or until you can smell spices.

Add beef stock and tomatoes. Bring to boil, stirring occasionally. Reduce heat and simmer for 45 to 60 minutes or until meat is tender.

Add beans and simmer for 10 minutes. Season well with salt and pepper.

MEXICAN RICE CASSEROLE

SERVES 4 TO 6

Essentially this is chili with rice cooked into it. It is a good one-dish meal for the family. Buy a good-quality tomato sauce or make your own.

2 tbsp vegetable oil
1 onion, chopped
1 clove garlic, chopped
1/2 green pepper, diced
1 red pepper, diced
1 lb lean ground beef
2 tbsp chili powder
Salt and freshly ground pepper to taste

1/2 jalapeño pepper, chopped
1 tbsp ground cumin
2 tsp dried oregano
1 cup corn kernels
2 cups tomato sauce
2 cups water
1 1/2 cups uncooked long-grain rice
1/4 cup chopped fresh coriander or parsley

Heat oil in large deep skillet on medium-high heat. Sauté onion, garlic, peppers, beef and chili powder for 1 minute. Season with salt and pepper.

Stir in jalapeño, cumin, oregano, corn and tomato sauce. Add water and bring to boil. Simmer 5 minutes. Scatter in rice.

Reduce heat to low, cover and simmer for 25 minutes or until rice is cooked. Stir in coriander. Taste and adjust seasonings.

CHILI POWDER

Chili powder is usually a mixture of chilies, cumin and other seasonings. Pure chili powder, which is just ground dried chilies, has much more flavor. Depending on the chili used, the heat will vary. New Mexican or ancho chili powders are the mildest, while pasilla is one of the hottest. Pure chili powders are usually available at Latin American or Mexican stores.

SKILLET BEEF SMOTHERED WITH ROOT VEGETABLES

SERVES 4

A winter dish for lovers of root vegetables. Make it with ground turkey or chicken, too.

1 tbsp olive oil	1 cup diced rutabaga
1 lb lean ground beef	1 cup diced potato
1 tsp dried thyme	1 cup diced sweet potato
Salt and freshly ground pepper to taste	2 cups beef stock
1 onion, chopped	1 tbsp tomato paste
1 cup diced carrot	1 tsp Worcestershire sauce
1 cup diced parsnip	. . . . .

Heat oil in large skillet on medium heat. Add beef, thyme, salt and pepper. Sauté until lightly browned, about 4 minutes. Remove beef from skillet.

Add onion, carrot, parsnip, rutabaga, potato and sweet potato to skillet. Sauté until coated with oil, about 2 minutes.

Stir in stock, tomato paste and Worcestershire. Return meat, bring to boil, cover and simmer gently for 30 minutes or until vegetables are cooked. Taste for seasoning, adding salt and pepper as needed.

SOUTH AMERICAN CREOLE STEW

SERVES 4 TO 6

A great stew with lots of healthy ingredients. Serve with rice, salad and hot pepper sauce.

1 tbsp vegetable oil

1 lb lean ground beef

Salt and freshly ground pepper to taste

1 onion, chopped

1 sweet potato, peeled and diced

1 red pepper, diced

1 jalapeño pepper, seeded and chopped

4 cloves garlic, chopped

pinch cinnamon

pinch ground cloves

2 cups canned tomatoes, chopped

1 cup beef stock

1 tbsp Worcestershire sauce

2 zucchini, diced

1 19-oz (540 mL) can white beans, drained and rinsed

3 tbsp chopped parsley

· · · · ·

Heat oil in large skillet on medium heat. Add beef, salt and pepper and sauté until beef loses its pinkness, about 4 minutes. Remove from skillet.

Add onion, sweet potato, peppers, garlic, cinnamon and cloves to skillet. Sauté for 2 minutes. Add tomatoes, stock and Worcestershire sauce.

Bring to boil and reduce heat to medium-low. Return meat, cover and simmer for 20 minutes.

Add zucchini and beans and simmer for 10 minutes or until vegetables are tender. Taste for seasoning, adding salt and pepper as needed. Stir in parsley.

BEEF AND BARLEY SKILLET SUPPER

SERVES 4

A healthy, easy one-dish meal. You can substitute other ground meat such as turkey if you wish.

1 tbsp olive oil	2 cloves garlic, chopped
1 lb lean ground beef	2 carrots, diced
1 tsp dried thyme	3 zucchini, diced
pinch hot red pepper flakes	1 cup uncooked pearl barley
Salt and freshly ground pepper to taste	1 tbsp soy sauce
1 onion, chopped	3 cups boiling beef stock or water
1 red pepper, diced	¼ cup chopped parsley

Heat oil in large deep skillet on medium heat. Add beef, thyme, hot pepper flakes, salt and pepper. Sauté beef until browned, about 2 minutes.

Add onion, red pepper, garlic, carrots and zucchini. Combine with meat and sauté for 2 minutes. Add barley and soy sauce and mix with meat and vegetables.

Add boiling stock to skillet and stir together. Bring to boil, cover and cook on low heat for 45 minutes or until barley is tender, adding more liquid if dish becomes too dry. Taste and adjust seasoning. Sprinkle with parsley before serving.

HERBED VEAL CHOPS

SERVES 4

Serve with an arugula salad for a perfect main course. If the thick veal rib chops are not available, use veal loin chops or pork rib chops.

4 veal rib chops, about 1½ inches thick

2 tbsp olive oil

2 tsp chopped fresh basil

2 tsp chopped fresh rosemary

2 tsp chopped fresh thyme

2 tsp grated lemon rind

Salt and freshly ground pepper to taste

• • • • •

Scrape veal bones clean and place chops on platter. Combine oil, basil, rosemary, thyme and lemon rind and brush on chops. Season with salt and pepper. Marinate for 1 hour at room temperature or up to 12 hours in refrigerator.

Grill or broil chops 4 to 6 minutes per side on high heat, depending on thickness of chops. They should be slightly pink. Remove from grill and serve.

PORK AND PEPPERS

SERVES 4

A quick dish that is both attractive and tasty. Substitute any vegetables you prefer but make sure they are cut the same size for even cooking.

3 small onions	1 red pepper, cut in 1-inch pieces
2 tbsp olive oil	1 yellow pepper, cut in 1-inch pieces
2 10-oz pork tenderloins	2 small zucchini, cut in 1-inch pieces
Salt and freshly ground pepper to taste	1 cup white wine
2 tsp chopped fresh rosemary	1 cup apple juice
or ¾ tsp dried	1 tsp red currant jelly

Peel onions and cut each into eight sections through the root.

Preheat oven to 350 F.

Heat oil in large skillet on medium heat. Brown pork on all sides, about 5 minutes. Remove to baking dish large enough to hold pork and vegetables. Season meat with salt, pepper and rosemary.

Add onions, peppers and zucchini to skillet and sauté until slightly brown and crisp-tender, about 5 minutes. Surround pork with vegetables in baking dish and pour in wine.

Bake, uncovered, for 25 minutes or until pork juices are no longer pink.

Pour wine and pan juices into skillet, add apple juice and bring to boil. Boil until reduced by half. Stir in red currant jelly and simmer for 1 minute.

Slice pork into thin slices, pour over sauce and garnish with vegetables.

MAPLE-GLAZED PORK CHOPS

SERVES 4

Use fairly thick pork chops for a juicy texture. Serve this with Cucumber Tomato Relish and Sweet Potato Puree (page 157).

1 tbsp vegetable oil	1 tbsp white vinegar
4 rib pork chops, about 1 inch thick	¼ cup maple syrup
Salt and freshly ground pepper to taste	½ tsp dry mustard
¾ cup tomato juice	• • • • •

Preheat oven to 350 F.

Heat oil in heavy skillet on high heat. Brown pork chops on both sides, about 2 minutes per side. Season with salt and pepper. Place in ovenproof casserole that holds chops in one layer.

Combine tomato juice, vinegar, maple syrup and mustard. Pour over chops. Cover and bake for 35 minutes. Uncover and bake for 10 minutes longer, until pork chops are tender and sauce thickens slightly.

CUCUMBER TOMATO RELISH

Combine 2 seeded and diced tomatoes, 1 cup diced seedless cucumber, ¼ cup chopped fresh basil, 1 tbsp rice vinegar, 2 tbsp olive oil and 2 tbsp chopped green onion. Season with salt and pepper.

Makes about 3 cups.

SWEET AND SOUR PORK CHOPS

SERVES 4

Another family favorite. Serve with rice and stir-fried vegetables.

½ tsp dried thyme	2 cups drained and chopped
Salt and freshly ground pepper to taste	canned tomatoes
4 rib pork chops, about 1 inch thick	¼ cup cider vinegar
1 tbsp vegetable oil	2 tbsp brown sugar
¼ cup red wine	1 tsp Dijon mustard

Sprinkle thyme, salt and pepper on pork chops.

Heat oil in skillet on medium heat. Add pork chops and brown fat side down for 1 minute. Brown each side for about 2 minutes per side.

Remove chops and discard fat. Add wine to skillet and bring to boil. Add tomatoes, vinegar, sugar and mustard. Return to boil.

Return pork chops to skillet, cover and simmer on medium-low for about 45 minutes or until pork is tender.

Taste for seasoning, adding more sugar, vinegar or seasonings as required.

BRAISED PORK TENDERLOIN WITH APPLES

SERVES 4

I like to use McIntosh apples in this dish because they fall to applesauce when cooked. If you prefer a chunky sauce, use Spys. You can substitute pork chops for the tenderloin, but increase the cooking time by 15 minutes.

2 tbsp butter	1 tbsp cider vinegar
1 lb pork tenderloin	½ tsp Dijon mustard
½ cup chopped onion	3 apples, peeled, cored and
½ tsp dried rosemary	coarsely chopped
½ cup apple juice	• • • • •

Heat butter in skillet on medium-high heat. When it is sizzling, add pork tenderloin. (If it does not fit in skillet, cut in half.) Sear meat for 2 to 3 minutes per side. Remove tenderloin, reserve and reduce heat to medium-low.

Add onion and rosemary to skillet and sauté for 5 minutes or until onion is softened. Add apple juice and vinegar, scraping up any bits in pan. Add mustard.

Raise heat and cook for 2 to 3 minutes or until mixture has reduced by half.

Add apples and tenderloin to pan. Lower heat to medium and simmer gently for 20 minutes or until pork is firm and no longer pink. Slice and serve with the apple mixture on the side.

PORK TENDERLOIN WITH APRICOT ALMOND STUFFING

SERVES 4

A good company meal. Serve with basmati rice.

1 1-lb pork tenderloin, butterflied
2 tbsp butter
1 small onion, finely chopped
6 dried apricots, chopped
¼ cup almonds, toasted (page 51) and chopped
½ cup fresh breadcrumbs
1 egg, beaten

¼ tsp paprika
1 tbsp chopped fresh thyme or 1 tsp dried
Salt and freshly ground pepper to taste
¼ cup white wine
1½ cups chicken stock
4 dried apricots, slivered
¼ cup whipping cream
. . . . .

Cover meat with plastic wrap and pound until about ½ inch thick.

Melt 1 tbsp butter in skillet over medium-high heat. Sauté onion for 2 minutes or until softened. Remove from heat.

Add chopped apricots, almonds, breadcrumbs, egg, paprika, thyme, salt and pepper to skillet. Stir together.

Place stuffing down center of tenderloin. Tie or skewer together.

Melt remaining 1 tbsp butter in clean skillet on medium-high heat. When sizzling, add tenderloin. Cook for 1 minute per side or until brown. Remove.

Add wine and chicken stock to skillet, scraping up any brown bits that remain on bottom of pan. Bring to boil.

Return pork to pan. Reduce heat to medium-low, cover and gently simmer for 20 to 25 minutes or until tender.

Remove pork to platter and keep warm. Bring sauce to boil and add slivered apricots and cream. Simmer for about 2 minutes or until slightly thickened.

Slice pork and serve with sauce spooned over top.

BUTTERFLYING PORK TENDERLOIN

To butterfly pork tenderloin, cut the tenderloin horizontally, about three-quarters of the way through to the other side. Open up the tenderloin and press flat.

CITYLINE LAMB CHOPS

SERVES 4

Lamb chops can dry out easily, so it is important not to overcook them.

1 clove garlic, chopped	3 tbsp chopped red onion
3 tbsp chopped fresh basil or mint	1 tbsp lime juice
1 tsp grated lime rind	2 tbsp Dijon mustard
1 tbsp soy sauce	1 tbsp chutney
2 tbsp olive oil	1/2 cup chicken stock
8 rib or loin lamb chops	• • • • •

Combine garlic, 1 tbsp basil, lime rind, soy sauce and 1 tbsp olive oil in small bowl. Brush on lamb chops. Marinate for 30 minutes or up to 2 hours.

Heat remaining 1 tbsp oil in non-stick skillet on medium-high heat. Add chops and cook for 3 to 4 minutes per side or until medium-rare. Remove chops from skillet.

Add onion, lime juice, mustard, chutney and stock to skillet. Bring to boil. Stir in remaining 2 tbsp basil. Serve sauce with chops.

RACK OF LAMB WITH ARUGULA AND ROSEMARY VINAIGRETTE

SERVES 4

A less traditional, light lamb preparation. If arugula is unavailable, use spinach or watercress.

2 lamb racks

2 tbsp butter, at room temperature

1 clove garlic, crushed

Grated rind and juice of 1 lime

2 tbsp chopped fresh rosemary

Salt and freshly ground pepper to taste

1 bunch arugula

1 tbsp balsamic or wine vinegar

3 tbsp olive oil

¼ cup chopped chives

Scrape away fat and meat from last 2 inches of bones. Trim off remaining fat.

Beat together butter, garlic, lime rind and juice, rosemary, salt and pepper. Spread over lamb racks. Marinate for 1 hour.

Preheat oven to 400 F.

Place lamb on rack in roasting pan. Roast for 30 to 45 minutes or until juices run pink. (Roast 15 to 20 minutes longer for medium.)

Place arugula in bowl.

Whisk together vinegar, olive oil and chives. Pour over arugula and toss well.

Slice lamb into chops. Place arugula salad on serving plates. Top with lamb chops. If there is any accumulated juice, pour over chops.

COOKING LAMB RACKS

Lamb racks come in different weights and sizes and are available both fresh and frozen. (Defrost frozen racks overnight in the refrigerator.) The smaller New Zealand lamb racks take 20 to 25 minutes in the oven at 400 F for rare; thicker North American racks take longer.

RACK OF LAMB WITH MUSTARD MINT TOPPING

SERVES 4

Serve this with Swiss chard and a grain of choice.

2 lamb racks	2 tbsp soy sauce
3 tbsp Dijon mustard	1/2 cup red onion, finely chopped
1/4 cup chopped fresh mint	1/2 cup red wine
or 1 tbsp dried	2 cups beef or chicken stock
2 tbsp olive oil	2 tbsp mint or apple jelly

Trim racks of fat. Scrape fat and meat from ends of bones. Heat large skillet on medium-high heat and fry racks fat side down for 3 minutes. Fry remaining sides for 3 minutes per side until outside is brown.

Combine mustard, mint, oil and soy sauce. Spread over racks and marinate for 30 minutes.

Preheat oven to 400 F.

Place lamb fat side up on wire rack in baking dish. Roast for 15 to 25 minutes, depending on thickness of rack, until pink. Let lamb sit for 10 minutes while making gravy.

Pour fat out of pan, leaving about 1 tsp. Heat on stove on medium-high heat. Add onion and sauté until softened, about 2 minutes.

Pour in wine and bring to boil. Add stock and mint jelly. Bring to boil and cook for 2 minutes or until sauce has thickened slightly.

Carve lamb into chops and serve with sauce.

HONEY-GLAZED EASTER LAMB

SERVES 6

Serve with new potatoes, steamed green beans and sautéed apples seasoned with a sprinkling of mint sauce. Either buy lamb already boned and butterflied or ask your butcher to do it for you. Because the roast is flat, it does not require a long cooking time.

¼ cup Dijon mustard	Salt and freshly ground pepper to taste
2 tbsp honey	1 3-lb boneless leg of lamb, butterflied
1 tbsp chopped garlic	1 tbsp all-purpose flour
1 tbsp grated lemon rind	2 cups beef stock
2 tbsp chopped fresh rosemary	1 tsp tomato paste
or 2 tsp dried	• • • • •

Combine mustard, 1 tbsp honey, garlic, lemon rind, rosemary, salt and pepper. Spread over lamb leg. Marinate for 2 hours.

Preheat oven to 450 F.

Place lamb on rack in roasting pan and bake for 15 minutes. Reduce heat to 350 F and bake for 20 to 30 minutes longer for medium-rare. Place lamb on a carving board and let rest for 10 minutes.

Discard all but 1 tbsp fat from roasting pan. Stir in flour. On medium heat, cook flour until browned, stirring.

Pour in stock, tomato paste and remaining 1 tbsp honey. Bring to boil, stirring. Simmer until reduced by half. Season well.

Carve lamb against the grain into thin slices and serve with gravy.

GRILLED BOMBAY LAMB

SERVES 6

Curry paste is available at the supermarket and it comes in different heats. If it is unavailable, use 2 tsp curry powder mixed with 2 tbsp vegetable oil.

Serve this with a tomato and onion salad and Coriander Chutney. To roast this lamb instead of grilling, follow the recipe for Honey-glazed Easter Lamb (page 117). Garnish with lime wedges and cherry tomatoes.

1 3-lb boneless leg of lamb, butterflied

2 tbsp chopped ginger

3 cloves garlic, chopped

2 tbsp curry paste

1/2 cup plain yogurt

· · · · ·

Trim fat from lamb.

Combine ginger, garlic, curry paste and yogurt in food processor or by hand. Spoon marinade on lamb and marinate for 6 hours or overnight in refrigerator.

Preheat grill to high. Place lamb fat side down on grill and sear for 3 minutes. Turn and sear second side for 3 minutes. Close lid, reduce heat to medium and grill for 10 minutes. Turn again and grill for 10 minutes until medium-rare.

Remove lamb, let rest for 10 minutes, then carve against the grain into thin slices.

CORIANDER CHUTNEY

You can buy this at Indian and Asian food stores, but making your own is easy. In food processor place a coarsely chopped bunch of coriander, 1 tsp chopped hot green chili or 1/4 tsp cayenne, 1 tbsp chopped ginger, 2 chopped cloves garlic, 1/2 cup thick coconut milk or plain yogurt, 1 tsp garam masala or curry powder, salt and lemon juice to taste. Process until smooth.

Makes about 1/2 cup.

CHAPTER 7

Pastas, Grains and Beans

And called it Macaroni.
—"Yankee Doodle Dandy"

PASTA WITH TANGY TOMATO SAUCE

SERVES 2

The anchovies disappear in the sauce but add a subtle flavor. Serve with Parmesan cheese.

8 oz pasta

2 tbsp olive oil

2 anchovies, finely chopped

1 28-oz (796 mL) can tomatoes, drained

1 tsp dried basil

½ tsp hot red pepper flakes or cayenne

1 cup chopped olives, artichokes

or tuna, optional

Salt and freshly ground pepper to taste

· · · · ·

Heat large pot of salted water until boiling. Add pasta and cook until *al dente*, 10 to 15 minutes depending on size of pasta.

Add oil to skillet on medium heat. Stir in anchovies. Add tomatoes, crushing them slightly as you stir them in. Add basil and hot pepper flakes. Bring to boil and simmer vigorously for 10 to 15 minutes or until thickened.

Stir in olives and cook until heated through. Season well with salt and pepper.

Drain pasta and serve with sauce.

PARMIGIANO REGGIANO

Parmigiano Reggiano is the finest Parmesan cheese. Its depth of flavor and nutty, fragrant taste make it a wonderful cheese for eating and cooking. It melts beautifully and binds together other ingredients. Grate it as you need it because it loses some of its flavor if it dries out. Avoid buying pre-grated Parmesan cheese in a can; it has no taste.

ORECCHIETTE WITH SPINACH WALNUT PESTO

SERVES 6 AS AN APPETIZER; 4 AS A MAIN COURSE

For an even stronger walnut flavor, toast the nuts before adding them to the sauce. You can use any short pasta (e.g., penne or farfalle), but orecchiette ("little ears") are perfect for holding the sauce.

1 bunch spinach, washed	2 cloves garlic, chopped
1 lb orecchiette	1/2 cup olive oil
1/2 cup chopped fresh basil or parsley	1/2 cup grated Parmesan cheese
1/4 cup walnuts, toasted (page 51)	Salt and freshly ground pepper to taste

Bring large pot of salted water to boil. Add spinach and cook for 2 minutes. Remove with slotted spoon. Spinach should be just wilted. Drain well and squeeze out as much water as possible. (There should be about 1 cup.)

Add orecchiette and boil until *al dente*, about 12 minutes. Drain, reserving about 1/4 cup pasta cooking water.

Add spinach to food processor or blender and combine with basil, walnuts and garlic. With machine running, add olive oil.

Stir in Parmesan, salt and pepper.

Toss orecchiette with spinach mixture and enough pasta water to thin sauce slightly.

PASTA SHAPES

Different shapes of pasta suit different sauces. Long, thin pastas such as spaghettini or angel-hair need light sauces that do not overpower the pasta. Thicker or wider pastas such as fettuccine or tagliatelle can handle heavier sauces (such as tomato sauces). Sauces that have chunks of meat or vegetables in them are best with short pastas such as penne or fusilli. As a rule of thumb, decide whether all the ingredients will stick to long pasta when it is twirled on a fork; otherwise serve the sauce with a short pasta.

LINGUINE WITH SAUSAGE AND MUSHROOMS

SERVES 4

This sauce is excellent with long pasta; however, if you slice the sausage into chunks, use a short pasta such as penne.

2 tbsp olive oil	¼ cup red wine
2 cloves garlic, chopped	1 28-oz (796 mL) can tomatoes,
1 small red onion, chopped	chopped, with juices
12 oz sweet Italian sausage, removed	1 tsp dried oregano
from casings and crumbled	Salt and freshly ground pepper to taste
8 oz shiitake mushrooms,	1 lb linguine
stemmed and sliced	2 tbsp chopped parsley

Heat oil in skillet on medium-high heat. Add garlic, onion and sausage meat. Sauté for 3 minutes or until sausage loses its pinkness.

Add mushrooms and sauté until slightly limp, about 2 minutes. Add wine, tomatoes and oregano. Bring to boil and simmer for 15 minutes or until slightly thickened. Season with salt and pepper.

Bring large pot of salted water to boil. Add linguine and boil until *al dente*, about 10 minutes.

Drain pasta and toss with sauce and parsley.

PASTA WITH PEPPERY LEEK SAUCE

SERVES 4

A comforting pasta for a winter's evening. Serve Spiced Mushrooms on Country Bread (page 45) as a first course for a casual dinner party. Use a wide noodle such as tagliatelle, pappardelle or fettuccine for this dish.

1 lb pasta	½ tsp dried thyme
3 leeks, trimmed	pinch grated nutmeg
4 oz bacon, chopped	⅓ cup grated Parmesan cheese
½ cup white wine	Salt to taste
½ cup whipping cream	½ tsp cracked peppercorns (page 56)
1 tsp Dijon mustard	• • • • •

Bring large pot of salted water to boil. Add pasta and cook until *al dente*, 10 to 15 minutes.

Split leeks in half and wash well. Remove dark green leaves. Slice thinly.

Add bacon to skillet on medium heat and sauté until limp, about 4 minutes. Drain off fat, leaving 1 tbsp.

Add leeks and sauté until softened, about 5 to 7 minutes.

Add wine and cook until reduced by half. Add cream, mustard, thyme, nutmeg and 2 tbsp grated Parmesan. Bring to boil. Season with salt and cracked peppercorns.

Drain pasta and serve with sauce and remaining cheese.

SPAGHETTINI WITH BRUSCHETTA SAUCE

SERVES 6 AS AN APPETIZER; 3 TO 4 AS A MAIN COURSE

This sauce should only be made when tomatoes are at their peak. Mixed with an excellent extra-virgin olive oil and garden-fresh basil, they make a brilliant summer dish. The pasta should be very hot and the sauce very cold.

8 large tomatoes, peeled and seeded	Salt and freshly ground pepper to taste
²/₃ cup extra-virgin olive oil	1 lb spaghettini
¼ cup chopped fresh basil	½ cup grated Parmesan cheese
1 tsp red wine vinegar	· · · · ·

Cut tomatoes into chunks and place in large bowl. Toss with oil, basil, vinegar, salt and pepper. Marinate at room temperature for 2 hours.

Bring large pot of salted water to boil. Add spaghettini, return to boil and boil for 10 minutes, or until pasta is *al dente*. Drain.

Toss sauce and pasta together. Serve sprinkled with Parmesan.

PASTA WITH PEAS, BACON AND RICOTTA

SERVES 4

Suitable with fusilli, rigatoni or orecchiette, this creamy, practically instant sauce is a quick supper dish that appeals to both kids and adults.

1 lb pasta	1 cup ricotta cheese
4 oz bacon, slivered	1 tbsp butter, melted
3 green onions, chopped	Salt and freshly ground pepper to taste
1 cup small green peas	1/2 cup grated Parmesan cheese
1/4 cup chopped parsley	. . . . .

Bring large pot of salted water to boil. Add pasta and cook for 10 to 15 minutes or until *al dente.*

Place bacon in skillet on medium heat and cook until browned and crisp, about 5 minutes. Discard all but 1 tbsp fat.

Add green onions and peas to skillet and stir together. Cook until peas are warmed though.

Beat together parsley, ricotta and butter in large bowl.

Drain pasta and add to bowl. Toss with ricotta, then fold in bacon/pea mixture. Season with salt and pepper. Sprinkle with Parmesan.

PENNE WITH SPICED GARLIC TOMATO SAUCE

SERVES 4

An over-the-top pasta recipe for garlic and spice lovers. For the best flavor you should use all the oil in the recipe; however, in the interests of low fat, you can cut back to 3 tbsp.

1 lb penne	1 tsp hot red pepper flakes to taste
⅓ cup olive oil	Salt and pepper to taste
6 cloves garlic, thinly sliced	¼ cup chopped parsley
4 cups chopped fresh	Grated Parmesan cheese
tomatoes, (about 6 large) or	· · · · ·
2 28-oz (796 mL) cans, drained	

Bring large pot of salted water to boil. Add penne and cook for 10 minutes or until *al dente*.

Pour olive oil into large skillet on medium-low heat. Add garlic and simmer for 5 minutes or until softened but not brown.

Raise heat to medium-high and add tomatoes and hot pepper flakes. Cook until a sauce forms, about 5 to 8 minutes. Season well with salt and pepper.

Drain pasta and toss with sauce and parsley. Serve at once with Parmesan cheese.

PASTA WITH RAPINI AND SHRIMP

SERVES 6 AS AN APPETIZER; 4 AS A MAIN COURSE

Strongly flavored and quick, this is the perfect pasta dish. Use broccoli if rapini is unavailable.

2 bunches rapini	1 tsp hot red pepper flakes
1 lb penne	12 oz large shrimp, peeled
6 tbsp olive oil	1 tbsp red wine vinegar
6 cloves garlic, sliced	Salt and freshly ground pepper to taste

Bring large pot of salted water to boil. Cut rapini stems into 1-inch pieces. Add stems and leaves to water and boil for 2 minutes. Remove with slotted spoon and drain.

Add pasta to boiling water and cook until *al dente*, about 12 minutes.

Add ¼ cup oil to large deep skillet on medium heat. Stir in garlic and hot pepper flakes. Sauté until garlic is tinged with gold around the edges, about 2 minutes.

Add shrimp and rapini to skillet and sauté until shrimp is pink, about 3 minutes. Add vinegar, salt and pepper.

Drain pasta and add to skillet with ¼ cup pasta cooking water and remaining 2 tbsp oil. Toss well.

RAPINI

Rapini, or broccoli rabe, is a skinny, green-stalked vegetable with broccoli-like florets, which is used extensively in Italian cooking. It has a somewhat bitter, peppery taste and adds zest and a slightly nutty flavor to a mild dish. It should be blanched before being used in dishes; or try adding it to stuffings or serving it as a side dish.

Rapini should keep for a few days wrapped in a paper towel and stored in the crisper in the refrigerator.

NOODLES WITH SPICY PEANUT SAUCE

SERVES 2

Add cooked or raw vegetables and leftover cooked poultry or fish to this dish, if desired.

12 oz thin pasta noodles	1/2 cup chicken or vegetable stock or water
(e.g., capellini or rice noodles)	2 tbsp soy sauce
1/4 cup peanut butter	1 tbsp sesame oil
1 tsp Asian chili sauce	1 tbsp granulated sugar
or other hot sauce	1 tsp white vinegar

Bring large pot of salted water to boil. Add pasta and boil until cooked, about 3 to 5 minutes, depending on the noodle. Drain well.

Whisk together peanut butter, chili sauce, stock, soy sauce, sesame oil, sugar and vinegar. Adjust seasonings and toss with noodles.

Serve hot or at room temperature.

MEDITERRANEAN-STYLE VEGETABLE LASAGNE

SERVES 4

An excellent lasagne that doesn't take long to assemble if you use packaged precooked lasagne noodles. I find that a quick soak in hot water softens them slightly and helps the pasta to cook more evenly.

2 tbsp olive oil

1 large onion, diced

1 clove garlic, chopped

2 small zucchini, diced

1/2 large eggplant, peeled and diced

1 red pepper, diced

1 tsp dried basil

1/2 tsp hot red pepper flakes

1 28-oz (796 mL) can tomatoes, pureed with juices

1/4 cup black olives, pitted and sliced

1/4 cup chopped parsley

Salt and freshly ground pepper to taste

8 oz Fontina, provolone, mozzarella or Cheddar cheese, grated

1 cup grated Parmesan cheese

9 instant lasagne noodles (approx.)

Heat oil in large skillet over medium heat. Add onion and garlic and sauté for 2 minutes or until onion is softened slightly.

Add zucchini, eggplant and red pepper and cook for 5 minutes. Sprinkle with basil and hot pepper flakes.

Add tomatoes, stir together and simmer, covered, for 15 minutes.

Stir in olives and parsley and season with salt and pepper.

Preheat oven to 375 F.

Combine Fontina and Parmesan.

Oil 11 x 7-inch baking dish. Layer one-third of lasagne noodles, slightly overlapping. Spread with one-third of sauce, then one-third of cheese. Repeat two more layers, finishing with sauce and cheese.

Bake for 30 minutes or until sauce is bubbling and cheese has melted.

TOPLESS LASAGNE

SERVES 4 AS AN APPETIZER

An elegant first course to serve before a simple main course. Make the sauce first and keep warm while you are cooking the lasagne noodles. This is a good recipe for using freshly made lasagne noodles.

2 tbsp butter	pinch grated nutmeg
¼ cup finely chopped onion	1 lb asparagus, trimmed and
¼ cup white wine	peeled if necessary (page 146)
½ cup whipping cream	8 lasagne noodles
1 cup crumbled goat cheese or ricotta	¼ cup slivered chives
Salt and freshly ground pepper to taste	¼ cup grated Parmesan cheese

Heat butter in skillet on medium heat. Add onion and sauté until softened, about 3 minutes.

Add wine and cook until liquid is reduced to 1 tbsp. Add cream and bring to boil. Stir in goat cheese. Season with salt, pepper and nutmeg.

Bring large pot of salted water to boil. Add lasagne noodles and boil until *al dente*.

Bring large skillet of water to boil. Add asparagus and boil for 2 to 3 minutes or until crisp-tender. Drain.

Lay 2 lasagne noodles on each plate. Top with asparagus spears and sauce. Garnish with chives and grated Parmesan.

SQUASH RAVIOLI WITH SAGE AND GARLIC SAUCE

SERVES 4

An easy way to make your own ravioli is to use wonton wrappers now available at many supermarkets and Chinese grocery stores. The filling can be squash, sweet potato or any vegetable puree you like. (The squash filling also makes an excellent side dish.)

These can be assembled a day ahead, but they should be cooked just before serving. If you do not like sage, use parsley, mint or basil instead.

Hubbard or Kaboka squash is drier than butternut and has a better consistency for this dish.

1 Hubbard squash, halved and seeded	**SAGE AND GARLIC SAUCE**
1 tbsp olive oil	¼ cup olive oil
2 shallots, chopped	2 cloves garlic, chopped
1 tbsp finely chopped parsley	1 tsp grated lemon rind
2 tbsp grated Parmesan cheese	2 tbsp chopped fresh sage
Salt and freshly ground pepper to taste	1 tbsp chopped parsley
32 wonton wrappers	¼ cup grated Parmesan cheese
1 egg white, beaten	• • • • •

Preheat oven to 450 F.

Place squash cut side down on oiled baking sheet. Bake for 30 to 40 minutes or until tender. Cool and scrape out flesh. Puree in food processor or mash by hand. (You should have about 1½ cups puree.)

Heat 1 tbsp oil in skillet over medium heat. Add shallots and sauté until softened, about 2 minutes. Stir in squash, parsley and Parmesan and beat together. Season well with salt and pepper.

Lay 16 wonton wrappers on counter. Brush edges with egg white. Top each with 1 heaping teaspoon squash mixture. Place second wrapper on top and seal edges. Place on baking sheet and cover with damp towel.

Heat ¼ cup oil in large skillet on low heat. Add garlic and cook gently for 5 minutes. It should not brown. Add lemon rind, sage and parsley. Stir together for 1 minute.

Bring large pot of salted water to boil. Add ravioli and return to boil. Boil for 2 to 3 minutes or until wrappers are cooked. Drain and toss in skillet with sauce. Sprinkle with Parmesan.

RISOTTO

SERVES 4

The perfect, creamy rice dish that requires a good stirring arm and a particular kind of rice (page 134).

5 cups (approx.) chicken stock

2 tbsp olive oil

2 tbsp butter

1/2 cup finely chopped onion

1 1/2 cups uncooked Carnaroli rice

1/4 cup grated Parmesan cheese

Salt and pepper to taste

2 tbsp chopped parsley

Bring stock to simmer on stove.

Heat large heavy pot on medium heat. Add olive oil and 1 tbsp butter. Add onion and sauté for 1 minute. Add rice and sauté until grains are coated with oil, about 2 minutes.

Add 1 cup stock to pot, cooking and stirring until the liquid is absorbed. Continue adding stock 1/2 cup at a time, stirring frequently, until rice is creamy with a slight bite in the center, about 20 minutes.

Remove from heat and stir in remaining 1 tbsp butter and Parmesan cheese. Season well with salt and pepper. Mound in soup plates, shaking them slightly until rice evenly coats the bottom of plate. Sprinkle with parsley and serve at once. Risotto waits for no one.

MUSHROOM RISOTTO

Slice 8 oz mixed wild mushrooms and sauté with onion. You can also soak 1/2 oz dried porcini mushrooms in water. Use the strained mushroom soaking liquid as part of the stock and add the soaked mushrooms to the fresh ones.

RADICCHIO AND RED WINE RISOTTO

Slice 1 head radicchio and sauté with onion until softened. Replace 1 cup stock with 1 cup red wine.

SPICED ZUCCHINI RICE

SERVES 4

An easy vegetable rice dish. You can add carrots, peas, green beans or other vegetables and omit the zucchini. Serve with curries. If basmati is not available, use regular long-grain rice.

2 green zucchini	3 cardamom pods, crushed, optional
1 yellow zucchini	2 cups uncooked basmati rice,
2 tbsp butter	soaked for 30 minutes and drained
1 onion, sliced	3 cups water
1 tsp cumin seeds	Salt to taste
1 2-inch cinnamon stick, broken in pieces	2 tbsp chopped fresh coriander
4 cloves	• • • • •

Slice zucchini into quarters lengthwise. Cut into ¼-inch slices.

Heat butter in heavy pot on medium heat. Add onion and sauté for 3 minutes. Add zucchini and sauté for 2 minutes.

Stir in cumin, cinnamon, cloves and cardamom. Sauté for 1 minute.

Add rice and sauté for 1 minute. Stir in water and salt. Bring to boil and boil until water has almost evaporated. Cover and leave on lowest heat for 10 minutes or until rice is tender.

Serve garnished with coriander.

PIQUANT MUSHROOM RICE

SERVES 4

Use Thai-scented rice in this recipe if it is available; serve with Hunan Beef with Asparagus (page 100).

1½ cups uncooked long-grain rice	2 tbsp soy sauce
1 cup tomato juice	½ tsp Asian chili sauce or hot pepper sauce
1½ cups chicken stock or water	1 cup green peas
3 portobello mushrooms, stemmed and diced	Salt to taste
½ cup chopped green onions	2 tbsp chopped fresh coriander

Rinse rice with cold water. Drain well.

Combine rice, tomato juice, stock, mushrooms, green onions, soy sauce, chili sauce and peas in large pot. Bring to boil on high heat. Cover, reduce heat to low and cook for 15 to 20 minutes or until rice is tender. (If rice seems a little dry, add extra hot water.)

Season with salt and sprinkle with coriander.

RICE

There are different sizes and shapes of rice. Long-grain rice has a slender grain and is fluffier and lighter than short-grain when cooked. Basmati is a long-grain Indian rice with a slightly nutty flavor. It should be soaked before cooking but requires less cooking liquid than other long-grain rices. Thai-scented long-grain rice is moist and tender when cooked but not fluffy. It has a subtle perfumed scent.

Converted rice has been parboiled. It is traditionally used in Caribbean dishes and jambalaya. The grains remain separate after cooking.

Short-grain rice is used for rice puddings. Arborio, Vialone Nano and Carnaroli are specialty short-grain rices used for making risotto. (Carnaroli is the one I prefer; it has lots of soft starch for a creamy consistency but retains a good firm bite when cooked.)

COCONUT RICE AND PEAS

SERVES 4

Not a true Caribbean rice and peas, but a lively side dish. If you are using fresh peas, you will need about 1½ lb unshelled peas.

1½ cups uncooked long-grain rice	1 cup peas
2¼ cups water	1 tsp chopped fresh thyme or pinch dried
½ cup coconut milk	Salt and freshly ground pepper to taste

Rinse rice with cold water.

Combine rice and water in pot. Bring to boil, cover and simmer for 15 minutes.

Add coconut milk, peas and thyme. Simmer for 5 minutes or until rice is cooked. Season with salt and pepper.

MUSHROOM FRIED RICE

SERVES 3

A good side dish for stir-fries.

2 tbsp vegetable oil	2 tbsp soy sauce
1 cup chopped onion	Salt and freshly ground pepper to taste
1 tsp grated ginger	2 eggs, beaten
8 oz mushrooms, sliced	1½ cups peas, fresh or defrosted
3 cups cooked rice	. . . . .

Heat oil in large skillet on high heat. Sauté onion and ginger until onion has softened, about 1 minute. Stir in mushrooms and cook just until limp, about 1 minute.

Add rice and soy sauce to skillet and stir well. Season with salt and pepper and continue to cook, stirring, until rice grains are coated in oil and soy sauce.

Add eggs and stir-fry with rice until cooked, about 2 minutes. Add peas and toss together.

PASTA WITH RAPINI AND SHRIMP (PAGE 127)

ROASTED VEGETABLES (PAGE 144)

CHICKPEA AND CARAMELIZED ONION COUSCOUS

SERVES 6 AS A SIDE DISH

A great vegetarian main course or side dish. Serve it with Chicken Tagine with Green Olives (page 89) for a Moroccan-style dinner.
   There are many ways to caramelize onions; this is just one of them.

3 onions, sliced

2 tbsp olive oil

1 tsp ground ginger

1 dried chili pepper or pinch cayenne

1 tsp turmeric

½ cup raisins

1 cup vegetable stock or water

1 19-oz (540 mL) can chickpeas, drained and rinsed

Salt to taste

3 cups couscous

2 tbsp chopped fresh mint

2 tbsp chopped fresh coriander

. . . . .

Place onions in large skillet on medium heat. Add oil, ginger, chili and turmeric. Add water to cover. Simmer until water evaporates and onions begin to brown.

Stir in raisins and continue to cook until onions are golden, about 10 minutes.

Stir in stock and chickpeas. Bring to boil and add salt. Cook for 5 minutes.

Cook couscous according to package directions.

Place couscous on large platter. Make a well in center and fill with onion/chickpea mixture. Sprinkle with mint and coriander.

QUICK COUSCOUS DINNER

Bring 1½ cups chicken or vegetable stock to boil. Stir in 1 cup quick-cooking couscous, 1 tsp ground cumin, ½ tsp paprika and salt and pepper to taste. Cover, remove from heat and let sit for 5 minutes. Uncover and stir with fork. Stir in leftover meat, fish, vegetables, canned chickpeas and/or raisins for a complete meal.

Serves 2.

BARLEY RISOTTO

SERVES 3 TO 4

Because barley cooks to a creamy consistency, it makes an excellent risotto, and it doesn't require constant stirring. Serve this with lamb or pork.

5 cups chicken stock or water	1 cup uncooked pearl barley
2 tbsp olive oil	Salt and freshly ground pepper to taste
1 small onion, chopped	2 tbsp chopped parsley
2 cloves garlic, chopped	1/2 cup grated Parmesan cheese
2 cups diced butternut or pepper squash	• • • • •

Heat stock in pot until simmering.

Heat oil in heavy pot on medium heat. Add onion and cook for 1 minute. Add garlic and sauté for 1 minute or until onion is softened.

Add squash and cook for 2 minutes. Stir in barley and sauté for 1 minute or until barley is coated with oil.

Add 1 cup stock, bring to boil and simmer, stirring occasionally, until barley absorbs most of stock. Add 2 more cups stock, cover and cook for 20 minutes or until most of stock has been absorbed.

Stir in 1 cup more stock and cook, uncovered, stirring frequently, until stock is absorbed, about 5 minutes. Add remaining stock and cook and stir until barley is tender, about 10 minutes longer. Season well with salt and pepper.

Beat in parsley and cheese. Serve immediately. Risotto thickens as it sits, but it can be reheated by beating in more stock or water.

POLENTA WITH SAUTÉED VEGETABLES

SERVES 4

Use your favorite vegetables in this recipe, or serve the polenta plain. Use as a side dish with Herbed Veal Chops (page 108)

4 cups chicken stock or water	4 oz green beans, trimmed and halved
1 cup polenta	1 tbsp olive oil
Salt and freshly ground pepper to taste	2 cloves garlic, sliced
½ cup grated Parmesan cheese	1 red pepper, sliced

Bring stock to boil in pot on medium heat. Slowly whisk in polenta. Lower heat and simmer for 15 minutes, stirring frequently, until polenta is thick. Season well with salt and pepper and beat in Parmesan.

Pour polenta into oiled 8-inch square baking pan and smooth top. Cool.

Preheat oven to 400 F.

Cut polenta into squares and place on oiled baking sheet. Bake for 15 minutes or until slightly browned.

Bring small pot of water to boil. Add beans and cook for 2 minutes. Rinse under cold water and reserve.

Heat olive oil in skillet on medium-high heat. Add garlic, red pepper and green beans. Sauté until peppers are softened and garlic is golden, about 5 minutes. Season well.

Serve polenta topped with vegetables.

POLENTA

Polenta is ground cornmeal. The cornmeal can be yellow or white and it comes in different textures, but coarse grain is best for polenta. It can be served soft and creamy like mashed potatoes or it can be chilled, sliced and fried. Polenta can also be baked in the oven. Use it to replace a starch in a meal.

Instant polenta has been precooked, dried and ground. It cooks in 5 minutes.

BRAISED LENTILS

SERVES 4

Cook lentils in vegetable or chicken stock for the most flavor. Don't worry if some stock remains after cooking—it just makes the lentils more creamy.

1 tbsp olive oil
1 onion, chopped
1 stalk celery, chopped
1 clove garlic, chopped
1½ cups dried green lentils

1 bay leaf
pinch dried thyme
Chicken or vegetable stock
or water (about 3 cups)
Salt and freshly ground pepper to taste

Place oil in pot on medium heat. Add onion, celery and garlic. Sauté until softened, about 2 to 3 minutes.

Add lentils to pot and sauté for 1 minute. Add bay leaf and thyme.

Cover lentils with stock by ½ inch. Bring to boil, cover and simmer for 35 minutes.

Uncover pot and cook for 5 minutes, stirring occasionally, until lentils are cooked. Season with salt and pepper.

LENTILS

Green or brown lentils are thin-skinned and require no soaking. They cook to a soft texture. French green or Le Puy lentils are smaller and darker green than green/brown lentils, and they have a deeper flavor. Red and yellow lentils are skinless; they turn a golden color and dissolve into a puree when cooked.

REFRIED BEANS

SERVES 4

This is a superb side dish—full of flavor. Serve with grilled chicken or pork dishes as well as Mexican ones.

1 1/2 tbsp vegetable oil or lard	3/4 cup chicken stock or water
1 small onion, chopped	dash hot pepper sauce or to taste
1/3 cup chopped smoked ham	Salt to taste
1 19-oz (540 mL) can kidney beans, drained and rinsed	2 tbsp chopped fresh coriander
	• • • • •

Heat oil in skillet on medium-high heat. Add onion and sauté until softened, about 2 minutes.

Add ham and beans and sauté for 5 minutes. Mash beans coarsely with potato masher.

Add stock and simmer gently, stirring occasionally, for 5 minutes or until beans thicken. Season with hot pepper sauce, salt and coriander.

VEGETARIAN CHILI

SERVES 4 TO 6

A healthy and substantial chili for the non-meat-eater. Include other vegetables if desired. Serve with warm tortillas, sour cream and chopped onion.

2 tbsp vegetable oil
1 red pepper, diced
1 jalapeño pepper, seeded and
     diced, optional
1 onion, chopped
4 cloves garlic, chopped
1 tsp ground cumin
1 tsp dried oregano
2 tbsp chili powder

¼ tsp hot red pepper flakes
2 cups diced squash
Salt and freshly ground pepper to taste
1 28-oz (796 mL) can tomatoes, with juices
2 medium zucchini, diced
1 19-oz (540 mL) can black beans
or kidney beans, drained and rinsed
¼ cup chopped parsley
• • • • •

Heat oil in large pot on medium heat and add peppers, onion and garlic. Cook until softened, about 5 minutes.

Add cumin, oregano, chili powder and hot pepper flakes and sauté for 1 minute.

Add squash and sauté until coated with spices. Season with salt and pepper.

Chop tomatoes and add to pot. Bring to boil. Reduce heat to medium-low and simmer for 10 minutes.

Add zucchini, beans and parsley and simmer for 10 minutes or until zucchini and squash are cooked through. Taste and adjust seasonings.

CHAPTER 8

Vegetables and Side Salads

Cauliflower is nothing but cabbage with a college education.
—Mark Twain

Roasted Vegetables

Roasted Asparagus

Celeriac Crisps

Caramelized Cabbage

Sweet and Sour Red Cabbage

Swiss Chard with Balsamic Mustard Glaze

Glazed Belgian Endive

Braised Fennel Italian Style

Stir-fried Watercress and Mushrooms

Spiced Squash and Leek Gratin

Carrot, Zucchini and Potato Nest

Zucchini and Red Pepper Compote

Potato and Mushroom Gratin

Roasted Sweet Potatoes

Really Roasted Potatoes

Rosti Potatoes with Caramelized Onions

Smothered Potatoes

Mum's Last Word in Latkes

Bistro Frites

Peppery Cucumber Salad

Lettuce Salad with Pears and Roquefort

Tomato Herb Salad with Sun-dried
    Tomato Toasts

Sweet Onion Salad

Low-fat Caesar Salad

Tomato Olive Salad

Tuscan Salad

Spinach Salad with Creamy Garlic Dressing

Fava Bean and Asparagus Salad

White Bean Salad

Herbed Barley Salad

Potato and Green Bean Salad

ROASTED VEGETABLES

SERVES 4

Almost all vegetables roast beautifully, and the roasting caramelizes the natural sugar, giving them a sweeter taste. Cut vegetables the same size for even cooking and an attractive presentation.

1 small butternut squash, peeled, seeded and cut in 2-inch pieces	1 onion, cut in 8 wedges
2 red peppers, seeded and cut in 2-inch pieces	4 plum tomatoes, halved
	1 tbsp chopped fresh thyme or 1 tsp dried
1 sweet potato, peeled and cut in 2-inch pieces	2 tbsp chopped fresh rosemary or 2 tsp dried
2 zucchini, cut in 2-inch pieces	¼ cup olive oil
1 eggplant, cut in 2-inch pieces	2 tbsp balsamic vinegar or lemon juice
	Salt and freshly ground pepper to taste

Preheat oven to 450 F.

Cut onion into 8 wedges. Cut off root end and separate onion pieces.

Place squash, peppers, sweet potato, zucchini, eggplant, onion and tomatoes in large bowl.

Add thyme, rosemary, oil, vinegar, salt and pepper to bowl and toss with vegetables. Place vegetables in single layer in roasting pan. Use 2 pans if necessary.

Roast vegetables for 35 to 40 minutes, stirring every 10 minutes, until cooked through and browned.

PASTA WITH ROASTED VEGETABLES

Toss cooked pasta with roasted vegetables. Serve with grated Parmesan and lots of black pepper.

ROASTED VEGETABLE CASSEROLE

Place roasted vegetables in casserole and top with grated Cheddar. Bake at 350 F until cheese melts and vegetables are hot.

ROASTED ASPARAGUS

SERVES 2

A favorite method for cooking asparagus. Serve it hot or cold with Orange Mint Vinaigrette.

1 lb asparagus, trimmed
2 tbsp olive oil
Salt and freshly ground pepper to taste

Preheat oven to 500 F.

Place asparagus on baking sheet and brush with oil.

Bake for 5 to 7 minutes or until crisp-tender. Season with salt and pepper.

ASPARAGUS

Look for bright-green, firm stalks and compact heads. Avoid feathery tips or stalks that are beginning to wilt. Store asparagus in the refrigerator and, if you are keeping it for more than a day, stand the stalks upright in about 1 inch of water.

Wash asparagus, then snap off the base of the stalks; don't cut them. Snapping the stalks naturally removes the tough, woody ends. Peel thicker stalks up to their heads with a vegetable peeler so they will cook more evenly; pencil-thin stalks do not need to be peeled. Choose stalks of similar size for even cooking.

Cooking time will vary according to the thickness of the stalks. Bring a skillet of water to boil, add asparagus and cook until crisp-tender, about 1 to 3 minutes. The asparagus should then be well drained and refreshed with cold water so it retains its color and texture.

ORANGE MINT VINAIGRETTE

Whisk together ½ cup mayonnaise, 2 tbsp orange juice, 1 tbsp lemon juice, 1 tsp grated orange rind and 2 tbsp chopped fresh mint. Spoon over 1½ lb cooked or roasted asparagus.

Serves 3 to 4.

CELERIAC CRISPS

SERVES 4

Substitute baking potatoes or sweet potatoes for different crispy tastes. The secret is to slice the vegetables as thinly as possible. Use the fine slicer on a food processor or a mandolin slicing machine. (Good plastic ones manufactured in Japan are easy to use. The large heavy French mandolins are best left to professionals.)

1 small celeriac, peeled
Salt and freshly ground pepper to taste
1 tsp chili powder
¼ cup olive oil

Preheat oven to 450 F.

Slice celeriac thinly in a food processor or with a mandolin. Season with salt, pepper and chili powder. Toss with oil.

Bake for 10 to 15 minutes, turning once, until brown and crisp.

CELERIAC

Celeriac, or celery root, is a gnarled root that has a strong celery-like flavor. It is a special variety of celery that is often pureed with other vegetables such as potatoes.

CARAMELIZED CABBAGE

SERVES 4 TO 6

A recipe that will change the minds of those who claim they don't like cabbage. This dish can be prepared ahead of time and reheated when needed.

2 tbsp butter	1 tbsp brown sugar
1 tbsp vegetable oil	4 cloves garlic, thinly sliced
1 head green cabbage, shredded	1 tbsp wine vinegar
(about 8 cups)	Salt and freshly ground pepper to taste

Heat butter and oil in large skillet on medium heat. Add cabbage, sugar and garlic. Sauté until cabbage is limp, about 5 minutes.

Add vinegar. Reduce heat to medium-low and continue to cook, stirring frequently, until cabbage becomes a golden color, about 20 minutes. Season well with salt and pepper.

SWEET AND SOUR RED CABBAGE

SERVES 8 TO 10

A family staple that goes well with all poultry and can be made up to a week ahead of time. Reheat in a covered pan in the oven or on top of the stove.

1 medium red cabbage	¼ cup red wine vinegar
3 tbsp vegetable oil or bacon fat	2 tbsp brown sugar
1 large red onion, chopped	3 cloves
1 large apple, peeled and chopped	1 tsp dried thyme
½ cup red wine	Salt and pepper to taste

Remove core from cabbage, cut in quarters and slice thinly. You should have about 8 cups.

Heat oil in heavy pot on medium heat. Add onion and sauté until softened, about 3 minutes.

Add cabbage and sauté until cabbage is coated with oil.

Add apple, wine, vinegar, sugar, cloves and thyme. Bring to boil, cover, reduce heat and simmer for 45 minutes or until cabbage is tender. Season well with salt and pepper.

SWISS CHARD WITH BALSAMIC MUSTARD GLAZE

SERVES 4 TO 6

A favorite side dish with lamb. I usually use light sour cream or yogurt in this dish.

1 large bunch Swiss chard

1 tbsp olive oil

3 cloves garlic, chopped

¼ cup sour cream or plain yogurt

1 tbsp Dijon mustard

2 tbsp balsamic vinegar

Salt and freshly ground pepper to taste

· · · · ·

Slice stalks and leaves of chard into 1-inch strips.

Heat oil in large skillet on high heat. Add chard stalks and sauté for 1 minute.

Add garlic, sauté 1 minute, then add chard leaves. Sauté until coated with oil, about 1 minute.

Reduce heat to medium-low, cover skillet and steam for 7 to 10 minutes or until chard is tender.

Combine yogurt, mustard and vinegar. Stir into chard. Simmer for 2 to 3 minutes or until chard has absorbed some of sauce. Do not bring mixture to boil because the sour cream will curdle. Season with salt and pepper.

SWISS CHARD

Swiss chard is either red- or green-stemmed, with broad, fleshy leaves. Look for crisp, fresh leaves with no sign of limpness. Cooked like spinach but with more flavor and texture, chard is wonderful served alone or in stuffings, quiches and egg dishes.

GLAZED BELGIAN ENDIVE

SERVES 4 TO 6

This elegant vegetable loses its slightly bitter taste when cooked. It has a silken texture and a luxurious flavor. To reheat, place in a baking dish, cover and reheat at 350 F for 15 minutes or until hot.

4 Belgian endives	2 tbsp chopped parsley
½ cup orange juice	2 tbsp butter
½ cup chicken stock or water	Salt and freshly ground pepper to taste

Cut endives in half lengthwise. Place in skillet large enough to hold them in one layer.

Pour orange juice and stock over endives. Sprinkle with parsley and dot with butter. Bring to boil, reduce heat to low and simmer gently for 25 to 30 minutes or until endives are soft. Season with salt and pepper.

BRAISED FENNEL ITALIAN STYLE

SERVES 4

Meltingly soft with a subtle licorice flavor. Substitute Belgian endive or leeks, if desired. Serve this with veal or chicken.

2 bulbs fennel	**2 tbsp butter**
Salt and freshly ground pepper to taste	**¹/₂ cup grated Parmesan cheese**
¹/₄ cup white wine	**· · · · ·**

Preheat oven to 400 F.

Cut tops off fennel. Cut each bulb into quarters and cut quarters in half.

Bring pot of salted water to boil. Add fennel and boil for 5 minutes or until slightly softened. Drain and place in oiled baking dish. Season with salt and pepper.

Pour wine over fennel and dot with butter. Sprinkle with cheese.

Bake for 20 minutes. Baste with juices and serve.

FENNEL

To prepare fennel, remove any brown outer leaves. Remove stalks and fronds. (The fronds can be saved for garnishing.) Cut fennel in half or quarters depending on size, or cut into slices. Raw or cooked, fennel adds a wonderful texture and slightly licorice taste to dishes.

STIR-FRIED WATERCRESS AND MUSHROOMS

SERVES 4

If you can find pea shoots, usually available in Asian markets, substitute them for the watercress.

2 bunches watercress	6 shiitake mushrooms, stemmed
1 tbsp vegetable oil	and thinly sliced
1 tsp grated ginger	1 tbsp soy sauce
1 tsp finely chopped garlic	2 tbsp chicken stock or water
2 green onions, finely chopped	Salt and pepper to taste

Trim 1 inch off base of watercress stalks.

Heat oil in skillet or wok on high heat. Add ginger, garlic and onions. Stir-fry for 30 seconds.

Add mushrooms and watercress and stir-fry until mushrooms have softened and watercress is wilted, about 2 minutes.

Add soy sauce and stock. Bring to boil and season with salt and pepper. Serve immediately.

SPICED SQUASH AND LEEK GRATIN

SERVES 6

Using Eastern Mediterranean spices in this squash dish gives it a whole new taste. Assemble it up to a day ahead of time and bake just before serving.

1 butternut squash, halved and seeded

2 tbsp butter

3 leeks, dark-green leaves removed, washed and thinly sliced

1 tsp ground cumin

1 tsp dried ground ginger

¹/₂ tsp cinnamon

pinch cayenne

¹/₄ cup whipping cream

Salt and freshly ground pepper to taste

2 tbsp chopped fresh coriander

. . . . .

Preheat oven to 450 F.

Place squash on oiled baking sheet cut side down and bake for 25 to 30 minutes or until soft. Cool and scrape squash off skin. Mash and reserve. Reduce oven to 350 F.

Heat butter in large skillet on medium heat. Add leeks and sauté until softened, about 5 minutes. Add cumin, ginger, cinnamon and cayenne and cook together for 1 minute.

Stir in squash and cream. Taste for seasoning, adding salt and pepper as needed. Place in oiled gratin dish.

Bake for 15 minutes. Garnish with coriander.

LEEKS

Slice leeks lengthwise to about 1 inch of root. Rinse between the leaves with warm water to dislodge any dirt. Remove strongly flavored dark-green leaves (discard or freeze to use in stocks).

CARROT, ZUCCHINI AND POTATO NEST

SERVES 4

An easy stir-fried dish that combines the starch and the vegetable all in one. It is colorful enough to brighten up any plate.

2 large Yukon Gold or baking potatoes, peeled

2 medium carrots, peeled

2 medium zucchini

2 tbsp butter

1 tbsp slivered fresh basil

Salt and freshly ground pepper to taste

· · · · ·

Grate potatoes by hand or in food processor. Rinse with cold water and drain well.

Grate carrots and zucchini.

Melt butter in large skillet on medium-high heat. When sizzling, add potatoes and carrots. Sauté for 2 minutes.

Add zucchini, basil, salt and pepper. Sauté for 2 minutes. Cover and simmer for 7 to 10 minutes or until vegetables are tender.

ZUCCHINI AND RED PEPPER COMPOTE

SERVES 4

For a vibrant color combination use both yellow and green zucchini. Make ahead of time and reheat when needed.

2 medium zucchini	2 tomatoes, finely chopped
2 tbsp olive oil	2 tbsp slivered fresh basil
1 red pepper, diced	Salt and freshly ground pepper to taste
1 clove garlic, chopped	· · · · ·

Cut zucchini in half lengthwise and slice.

Heat oil in skillet on medium-high heat. Add zucchini and red pepper and sauté until vegetables are browned and slightly softened, about 5 to 6 minutes.

Stir in garlic, tomatoes and basil and bring to boil. Season with salt and pepper.

POTATO AND MUSHROOM GRATIN

SERVES 4

An easy potato dish scented with mushrooms. Serve with Stuffed Turkey Breast (page 93) or Rack of Lamb with Mustard Mint Topping (page 116).

3 Yukon Gold or baking potatoes, peeled and thinly sliced	¼ tsp dried thyme
4 cloves garlic, peeled	½ cup whipping cream
1 cup milk	Salt and freshly ground pepper to taste
	8 shiitake mushrooms, stemmed and sliced

Preheat oven to 400 F.

Place potatoes and garlic in pot. Add milk and thyme. Add water until potatoes are just covered.

Bring to boil, then simmer until potatoes are crisp-tender, about 7 minutes. Remove potatoes with slotted spoon and place in bowl.

Reduce milk and water until 1½ cups remain, about 5 minutes. Blend with a hand blender or potato masher to crush garlic, then combine with cream.

Place half of drained potatoes in ovenproof baking dish. Season with salt and pepper. Place mushrooms over potatoes. Pour over half of milk mixture. Top with remaining potatoes and milk.

Bake for 35 to 45 minutes or until potatoes are golden-brown on top and most of liquid has evaporated.

ROASTED SWEET POTATOES

SERVES 4

Sweet potatoes are low in calories, full of vitamins and very versatile. Store them in a cool place but never refrigerate them because it will spoil their flavor. Serve with roast chicken, turkey, pork or veal. If sage is not your taste, use rosemary.

4 sweet potatoes	12 fresh sage leaves or 1 tsp dried
¼ cup olive oil	Salt and freshly ground pepper to taste
4 cloves garlic, sliced	· · · · ·

Preheat oven to 400 F.

Peel sweet potatoes and cut lengthwise into 3 or 4 slices.

Combine oil, garlic and sage in bowl. Add sweet potatoes and toss. Season with salt and pepper.

Place sweet potatoes in roasting pan and bake for 45 minutes, turning occasionally. They should be soft on the inside and crispy outside.

SWEET POTATO PUREE

Bake sweet potatoes at 350 F for 45 minutes. Scoop out pulp. Mash well and mix with enough whipping cream or sour cream to make a puree. Season with salt and pepper.

REALLY ROASTED POTATOES

SERVES 6

Having tested many ways of roasting potatoes, I've found that this old-fashioned Scottish method works the best. It gives the potatoes a fluffy interior and a crunchy, mouth-watering exterior.

3 lb Yukon Gold or baking potatoes, peeled
1/3 cup olive oil or duck or beef fat
2 tsp dried rosemary
Salt and freshly ground pepper to taste

Preheat oven to 400 F.

Cut potatoes in half. If they are large, cut in half again.

Place potatoes in pot and cover with cold water. Bring to boil and simmer for 7 minutes. Drain well.

Return potatoes to pot and shake over turned-off burner to dry and rough up exterior.

Pour oil into roasting pan large enough to hold potatoes in one layer. Heat oil in oven or on top of stove until hot.

Add potatoes to pan and turn until coated with oil. Sprinkle with rosemary, salt and pepper. Roast for about 1 hour, turning occasionally, until crisp and golden.

POTATOES

Yukon Gold potatoes have a sunny yellow interior and a fluffy texture. Best mashed, roasted, baked or French fried, they can replace more common baking potatoes such as Idahos or russets.

Red potatoes have a creamy interior and a more waxy texture than Yukon Golds. They are excellent boiled or used in potato salads.

ROSTI POTATOES WITH CARAMELIZED ONIONS

SERVES 4

Similar to a traditional Swiss rosti, this has a hidden layer of onions. Make them ahead of time and reheat in a 350 F oven for 10 to 15 minutes before serving.

3 Yukon Gold or baking potatoes	2 tsp granulated sugar
2 tbsp butter	Salt and freshly ground pepper to taste
2 large onions, thinly sliced	1 tbsp olive oil

Place potatoes in pot, cover with cold water and bring to boil. Simmer for about 10 minutes, or until potatoes are still firm but with some give. Peel potatoes and cool. Grate into bowl.

Heat skillet on medium-high heat and add butter. When it sizzles, add onions and sugar. Sauté until softened, about 2 minutes.

Reduce heat to medium-low and continue to cook until onions are browned, about 10 minutes. Remove from heat and season with salt and pepper.

Heat olive oil in non-stick skillet on medium-low heat. Press in half of potatoes, top with all of the onions and finish with remaining potatoes.

Fry for about 6 to 8 minutes or until golden. Flip potatoes over using two spatulas or turn out onto plate and return to pan uncooked side down. Fry for 5 to 6 minutes longer or until potatoes are golden and cooked through.

SMOTHERED POTATOES

SERVES 4

These homey, satisfying potatoes are good served with steaks and hamburgers.

1 tbsp olive oil	4 Yukon Gold or baking potatoes,
2 leeks, trimmed and sliced	peeled and cut in chunks
4 oz bacon, diced	Salt and freshly ground pepper to taste
1 red pepper, diced	2 tbsp chopped parsley
1 cup chicken stock or water	• • • • •

Heat oil in large skillet on medium heat. Add leeks, bacon and red pepper and sauté until bacon starts to crisp, about 3 to 4 minutes.

Add stock and potatoes. Bring to boil, reduce heat and simmer, covered, for 25 minutes or until potatoes are tender and slightly broken up. Stir occasionally to stop potatoes from sticking. Season with salt and pepper and stir in parsley.

FLUFFY PARSNIPS AND WALNUTS

Peel 2 lb parsnips and cook in water until tender. Drain and mash with about 3 tbsp butter or to taste, ½ cup buttermilk, a tiny grind of nutmeg and a scattering of grated orange rind. Season well with salt and pepper. Reheat in 350 F oven when needed and top with toasted walnuts or crisply fried bacon.

Serves 6.

STIR-FRIED WATERCRESS AND MUSHROOMS (PAGE 152)

INSTANT CRÈME BRÛLÉE (PAGE 187)

MUM'S LAST WORD IN LATKES

MAKES ABOUT 12 LATKES

My nephews Daniel and Julian love their mum's latke recipe at Hanukah. Light and crisp, these are best eaten right out of the skillet.

3 large Yukon Gold or baking potatoes, peeled	Salt and freshly ground pepper to taste
1 onion	2 tbsp all-purpose flour
1 egg	1/2 tsp baking powder
	Vegetable oil for frying

Grate potatoes and onion in food processor or by hand.

Squeeze out any excess liquid and transfer to bowl. Mix in egg, salt, pepper, flour and baking powder.

Heat a thin layer of oil in large, heavy skillet on medium-high heat. Drop in potato mixture by 2 tbsp and flatten with spoon. Fry on both sides until golden-brown and crisp, about 5 minutes. Continue frying in batches, adding oil as needed.

Drain on paper towels.

BISTRO FRITES

SERVES 4

These are the best fries imaginable. Do the first frying early in the day and refry just before serving.

4 Yukon Gold or baking potatoes, peeled
Vegetable oil for frying
Salt to taste

Cut potatoes into strips about ¼ inch thick. Pat dry with paper towel.

Heat oil in wok or deep-fryer to about 300 F. (The oil should bubble gently when you add potatoes.) Slide potatoes into oil and fry for about 7 minutes or until limp and cooked through but not colored. Drain on paper towels and reserve.

Reheat oil to 375 F or until a bread cube browns in 15 seconds. Refry potatoes in 2 or 3 batches until golden, about 2 to 3 minutes. Drain well on paper towels or in a strainer placed over a bowl. Season with salt and serve at once.

PEPPERY CUCUMBER SALAD

SERVES 4

Serve with smoked salmon as a first course or with any grilled or poached salmon dish.

1 seedless cucumber, thinly sliced

Salt

1/2 cup sour cream

1 cup chopped red onion

1 tbsp white vinegar

1/2 tsp ground cumin

1/4 cup chopped fresh coriander or dill

1 bunch arugula or watercress

Paprika to taste

Pepper to taste

Place cucumber slices in strainer. Sprinkle lightly with salt and let drain for 30 minutes. Wipe slices dry.

Combine sour cream, onion, vinegar, cumin and coriander in bowl. Toss with cucumber.

Make a bed of arugula. Place cucumber salad on arugula and dust with paprika and pepper.

CITYLINE'S SUPER SALAD DRESSING

Use this on any green or vegetable salad. You can also add 1 finely chopped clove garlic or 2 finely chopped shallots.

Whisk together 1 tsp Dijon mustard with 2 tbsp wine vinegar in a bowl. Very gradually whisk in 3/4 cup olive oil until the mixture thickens. Stir in 1 tbsp chopped fresh herbs and salt and pepper to taste.

Makes about 1 cup.

LETTUCE SALAD WITH PEARS AND ROQUEFORT

SERVES 6

If you peel the pears ahead of time, sprinkle them with lemon juice to help them retain their color.

2 tbsp sherry vinegar

1 tsp honey mustard

1/3 cup walnut or olive oil

Salt and freshly ground pepper to taste

8 cups lettuce such as arugula, frisee, Belgian endive, escarole

3 ripe pears, peeled and thinly sliced

3 oz Roquefort or other blue cheese, crumbled

Whisk together vinegar, mustard, oil, salt and pepper.

Place lettuce in bowl and toss with vinaigrette.

Mound lettuce on individual serving plates. Surround with pear slices and crumbled Roquefort.

MISO GINGER VINAIGRETTE

Serve over cooked or raw spinach, sliced cucumber, or steamed broccoli, asparagus or cauliflower.

Combine 1/4 cup light miso (page 26) with 1/4 cup rice vinegar, 1 tbsp grated ginger, 1 tsp granulated sugar, 1/2 tsp sesame oil and a few drops of hot pepper sauce.

Makes about 1/2 cup.

TOMATO HERB SALAD WITH SUN-DRIED TOMATO TOASTS

SERVES 6

This salad is spectacular when tomatoes are in season. If the tomatoes are quite acidic, you can omit the vinegar.

SUN-DRIED TOMATO TOASTS

6 slices Italian baguette, about ½ inch thick

3 tbsp olive oil

10 sun-dried tomatoes

2 cloves garlic, chopped

2 tbsp chopped fresh basil

Salt and freshly ground pepper to taste

½ cup crumbled goat cheese

TOMATO HERB SALAD

4 large tomatoes, sliced

1 small red onion, thinly sliced

¼ cup slivered fresh basil

Salt and freshly ground pepper to taste

¼ cup olive oil

1 tbsp balsamic vinegar

. . . . .

Brush bread slices with 1 tbsp olive oil. Toast or grill until golden on both sides.

Place sun-dried tomatoes in pot and cover with water. Bring to boil, then simmer for 5 minutes or until tomatoes are softened. Drain and chop finely and place in bowl. Stir in garlic, chopped basil and remaining 2 tbsp olive oil. Season well with salt and pepper. Reserve.

Preheat oven to 350 F.

Spread goat cheese on each slice of toast. Top with sun-dried tomato mixture. Bake for 7 to 9 minutes or until warmed through.

Lay fresh tomato slices on platter. Top with onion and scatter with slivered basil. Season with salt and pepper. Sprinkle on olive oil and balsamic vinegar.

Serve salad with toasts.

SUN-DRIED TOMATOES

Cut plum tomatoes in half, remove seeds and squeeze gently to remove any juice. Salt lightly and place on baking sheet cut side up. Bake at 200 F for 12 to 16 hours or until dry but not blackened. Store covered in olive oil or in an airtight container in the refrigerator.

SWEET ONION SALAD

SERVES 4

Similar to a dish I had in Tuscany, this is great served as a nibble before dinner or as a first course. Pile on thinly sliced Italian cornmeal baguête.

½ cup olive oil	3 tbsp chopped fresh sage or parsley
1 cup sweet onion (e.g., Vidalia or Spanish), thinly sliced	2 cloves garlic, slivered
½ cup coarsely chopped walnuts	4 oz Parmesan cheese
	Salt and freshly ground pepper to taste

Heat oil in skillet on low heat. Add onion, walnuts, sage and garlic. Cook gently for 2 minutes, stirring occasionally.

Shave very thin slices of Parmesan into serving bowl (using vegetable peeler or sharp knife). Add warm onion mixture and toss together gently. Season with a little salt and lots of pepper. Serve at room temperature.

LOW-FAT CAESAR SALAD

SERVES 6

This is a CityLine viewer favorite. It tastes like a Caesar minus the fat. Grill chicken breasts and serve alongside for a light dinner. Use the remaining dressing for another salad.

½ cup low-fat cottage cheese	3 tbsp olive oil
1 anchovy, chopped	2 tbsp grated Parmesan cheese
¼ cup skim milk	Salt and freshly ground pepper to taste
1 tbsp lemon juice	1 head Romaine lettuce, torn into pieces
1 clove garlic, chopped	½ cup croutons

Puree cottage cheese, anchovy, skim milk, lemon juice, garlic and olive oil in food processor until smooth. Stir in Parmesan. Season with salt and pepper.

Place Romaine in salad bowl. Toss with half of dressing. Sprinkle with croutons.

LOW-FAT CROUTONS

Cut bread slices into cubes. Place on baking sheet and bake at 400 F for 5 to 8 minutes, turning once.

TOMATO OLIVE SALAD

SERVES 6

This salad makes a lovely lunch served with a platter of prosciutto garnished with fresh figs.

2 bunches arugula

4 tomatoes, thinly sliced

1 red onion, chopped

1 tbsp lemon juice

⅓ cup olive oil

¼ cup slivered fresh basil

Salt and freshly ground pepper to taste

1 cup pitted black olives

Place arugula on platter. Cover with tomatoes and onion.

Whisk together lemon juice, olive oil, basil, salt and pepper. Pour dressing over salad and garnish with olives.

TUSCAN SALAD

SERVES 4

My favorite salad for a buffet. It's colorful, lively and great tasting. You can substitute ½ cup sliced pimentos for the grilled red pepper.

1 red pepper	2 cups croutons
1 Romaine lettuce, torn in pieces	2 tbsp red wine vinegar
1 small head radicchio, torn in pieces	½ cup olive oil
1 bunch arugula, torn in pieces	Salt and freshly ground pepper to taste
½ cup chives, cut in 3-inch lengths	2 oz Parmesan cheese
2 oz prosciutto, thinly sliced	• • • • •

Cut red pepper in half and remove seeds. Grill or broil until skin is black, about 5 minutes. Cool, then peel. Slice pepper into thin strips.

Toss together Romaine, radicchio, arugula, chives, red pepper, prosciutto and croutons in large bowl.

Whisk together vinegar and olive oil. Toss with salad. Season well with salt and pepper.

With vegetable peeler or sharp knife, shave Parmesan over salad.

SPINACH SALAD WITH CREAMY GARLIC DRESSING

SERVES 4 TO 6

Serve for lunch with Tomato Toasts on the side. The dressing is herbal and low-fat and should keep in the refrigerator for up to one week.

1 bunch spinach, torn in bite-sized pieces
1 small red onion, sliced
1 cup sliced mushrooms
1 orange, peeled and separated in segments
1/2 cup sprouts

CREAMY GARLIC DRESSING
2 cloves garlic, chopped
3/4 cup light sour cream
1/4 cup buttermilk
2 tbsp lemon juice
Salt and freshly ground pepper to taste
2 tbsp chopped fresh dill

Arrange spinach in salad bowl and top with onion, mushrooms, orange segments and sprouts.

Whisk together garlic, sour cream, buttermilk, lemon juice, salt, pepper and dill. Use half of dressing on salad and reserve remainder for another salad.

TOMATO TOASTS

Finely chop fresh tomatoes and mix with olive oil and salt and pepper to taste. Grill or toast slices of baguette and top with tomato mixture.

FAVA BEAN AND ASPARAGUS SALAD

SERVES 2

This salad was served to me at Lulu's Restaurant in San Francisco. It is a dynamic combination of asparagus, favas, chives and lemon.

8 oz asparagus	1 tbsp lemon juice
1 lb fava beans, peeled and skinned	Salt and freshly ground pepper to taste
(about ½ cup)	1 tbsp chopped chives
2 tbsp olive oil	1 oz Parmesan cheese, shaved

Bring skillet of water to boil. Add asparagus and cook until still crisp-tender, about 1 to 2 minutes. Drain and refresh with cold water.

Lay asparagus on platter. Sprinkle with fava beans.

Combine oil, lemon juice, salt and pepper. Drizzle dressing over salad. Sprinkle with chives. Using a vegetable peeler or sharp knife, shave thin slices of Parmesan over salad.

FAVA BEANS

Fava beans are used extensively in Mediterranean countries. They are often dried for winter consumption, reconstituted and mashed. Egyptians use them to make *ful*, a pureed bean dip similar to hummus. In Britain favas are known as broad beans.

Favas are labor-intensive to prepare, but they are a tender, earthy treat. Peel the large pods, removing the beans nestled inside. Bring a pot of water to a boil, toss in the beans and cook for 30 seconds. Drain and immediately immerse in ice water. Slip the tough outer skin from each bean and discard. The beans can now be eaten raw or lightly cooked.

Favas can be sautéed quickly in olive oil with a little prosciutto. They can be used in salads or simmered for a few minutes in broth. Or try folding them into risotto just before serving. If they are large, mash with butter or olive oil and Mediterranean seasonings.

1 lb fava beans in the pod = 1 cup shelled beans
1 cup shelled beans = ½ cup skinned beans

WHITE BEAN SALAD

SERVES 4

A fresh-tasting, minty salad that is excellent with chicken or seafood.

1 19-oz (540 mL) can white kidney beans, drained and rinsed	2 tsp Dijon mustard
2 cups diced seedless cucumber	1 clove garlic, finely chopped
1/2 cup chopped green onion	1/2 cup olive oil
1 cup chopped fennel or celery	1 tsp grated lime rind
3 tbsp lime juice	2 tbsp chopped fresh mint
	Salt and freshly ground pepper to taste

Combine beans, cucumber, green onion and fennel in bowl.

Whisk together lime juice, mustard and garlic. Slowly whisk in olive oil. Stir in lime rind and mint. Season with salt and pepper.

Toss beans and vegetables gently with dressing. Taste and adjust seasonings.

HERBED BARLEY SALAD

SERVES 6

A nutty-flavored grain salad with lots of crunchy, colorful vegetables. It keeps well for up to three days in the refrigerator.

3 cups water	6 green onions, chopped
3 cloves garlic, chopped	1/2 cup chopped radishes
1 cup uncooked pearl barley	1/2 chopped red pepper
2 tsp Dijon mustard	1/2 chopped yellow pepper
1 clove garlic, chopped	1/4 cup chopped parsley
1/4 cup red wine vinegar	1/4 cup chopped fresh basil
1/2 cup olive oil	2 tbsp chopped chives
Salt and freshly ground pepper to taste	· · · · ·

Combine water, garlic and barley in pot. Bring to boil.

Reduce heat, cover and simmer for 40 minutes or until barley is tender. Drain any excess water.

Whisk together mustard, garlic and vinegar. Slowly whisk in olive oil. Season with salt and pepper.

Combine half of dressing with warm barley. Cool.

Stir green onions, radishes, peppers, parsley, basil and chives. Toss with remaining dressing. Taste and adjust seasonings.

POTATO AND GREEN BEAN SALAD

SERVES 8

A colorful salad perfect for serving at a barbecue. Dress the potatoes while they are hot so they absorb the vinaigrette.

2 lb mini red potatoes	Salt and freshly ground pepper to taste
8 oz green beans, trimmed and halved	4 green onions, chopped
2 tbsp red wine vinegar	2 tbsp chopped parsley
2 tbsp lemon juice	1 tbsp chopped fresh tarragon
2 tbsp grainy Dijon mustard	or 1 tsp dried
3/4 cup olive oil	· · · · ·

Bring large pot of water to boil. Add potatoes and cook for 8 minutes. Add green beans to pot and cook for 2 minutes.

Drain potatoes and beans and place in large bowl.

Whisk together vinegar, lemon juice and mustard. Slowly beat in olive oil. Season with salt and pepper.

Toss potatoes and beans with dressing. Stir in green onions, parsley and tarragon. Taste and adjust seasonings.

CHAPTER 9

Desserts

I never worry about diets. The only carrots that interest me are the number you get in a diamond.
—Mae West

PEAR BISCOTTI

SERVES 4

A mouth-watering dessert based on a stunning combination of pears and biscotti. Serve it with whipped cream or ice cream.

5 tbsp butter	2 tsp grated lemon rind
½ cup brown sugar	1 tbsp lemon juice
3 large pears, peeled, cored and cut in 8 wedges	½ cup biscotti crumbs (about 3 large biscuits)

Preheat oven to 375 F.

Melt 3 tbsp butter in skillet on medium heat. Add sugar and cook for 2 minutes or until slightly foamy.

Add pears, lemon rind and juice. Sauté for 4 to 6 minutes or until pears are tender and sauce has reduced slightly.

Combine biscotti crumbs with remaining 2 tbsp butter. Place half of crumbs on bottom of buttered 4-cup soufflé or gratin dish. Top with pears and juice. Sprinkle with remaining crumbs.

Bake for 15 to 20 minutes or until golden-brown.

PEARS

Anjous are greeny-hued, egg-shaped pears with a sweet but slightly bland flavor. They are best used in cooking. Bartletts are yellow-green or deep red and are sweet and juicy. They are excellent eating pears, but their flavor and texture do not improve with cooking. Boscs are russet-colored pears with long slender necks, a buttery texture and tangy taste. They are good all-purpose pears for both eating and cooking, but they are not as juicy as Bartletts. Other good eating pears are Comice and Seckel.

BLUEBERRIES WITH CREAM

SERVES 4

Any berry can be used. Serve with dessert wafers, or wonton cookies (page 191).

1 cup whipping cream

½ cup drained plain yogurt (page 189)

2 tbsp lemon juice

2 tsp grated lemon rind

2 tbsp granulated sugar

4 cups fresh blueberries

Whip cream until it holds its shape.

Stir together yogurt, lemon juice, lemon rind and sugar.

Fold cream into yogurt mixture. Spoon into wine glasses alternating with layers of blueberries.

BERRY FRUIT SALAD

SERVES 6

Layer the fruit in a glass bowl for an attractive presentation. Spoon sauce over each layer (tossing the berries will spoil the effect) and garnish with slivered fresh mint leaves.

½ cup red currant jelly	3 cups sliced fresh strawberries
½ cup Port or sherry	2 cups fresh blueberries
1 tbsp finely chopped preserved	2 cups fresh raspberries
ginger in syrup	3 cups fresh cherries, pitted

Heat red currant jelly, Port and ginger in small pot on low heat until jelly dissolves.

Layer fruit in glass bowl, spooning sauce over each layer. Chill before serving.

SWEET AND SOUR STRAWBERRIES

Fill a small basket with fresh strawberries and serve with bowls of sour cream and icing sugar for dipping.

BERRY POPS

Crush 4 cups ripe strawberries or raspberries with sugar or honey to taste. Freeze in molds.

PEACHES WITH RASPBERRY SAUCE

SERVES 4

A fast raspberry-peach dish. Freestone peaches are the juiciest. Look for creamy-colored peaches that have a blush on the skin.

¼ cup raspberry jam	4 peaches, peeled and sliced
¼ cup apricot jam	4 cups vanilla ice cream
¼ cup Amaretto or brandy	1 cup slivered almonds, toasted (page 51)

Combine jams in large skillet. Cook on low heat until jams have dissolved.

Pour in Amaretto. Bring to boil, add peaches and stir together until peaches are warmed through.

Place ice cream on serving plates and top with peaches, sauce and almonds.

CARAMELIZED APPLES WITH CINNAMON ICE CREAM

SERVES 4

Flavor the ice cream with finely chopped preserved ginger or grated orange rind instead of cinnamon, if desired.

2 cups vanilla ice cream

1 tsp cinnamon

¹/₂ cup butter

¹/₂ cup granulated sugar

4 apples, peeled, cored and sliced

• • • • •

Soften vanilla ice cream in microwave or leave on counter. Beat in cinnamon and refreeze.

Heat butter and sugar in skillet on medium heat. Bring to boil, then simmer until sugar turns pale gold, about 3 minutes.

Add apples and cook until apples are tender and sauce is rich brown color.

Place ice cream in bowls and pour apples and sauce over top.

APPLES

Look for unblemished, brightly hued, firm apples, but don't press them too hard because they bruise easily. McIntosh apples turn to sauce when cooked. Mutsus, Spys and Red Romes hold their shape.

Store apples loose in the refrigerator. If you've picked a bushel of apples and want to store them over the winter, wrap the apples individually in newspaper and store in a cool, dark place.

GINGERED BANANAS

SERVES 4

For an extra treat, stir chopped preserved ginger into vanilla ice cream and serve with the bananas.

¼ cup butter	3 tbsp brown sugar
3 firm ripe bananas, peeled and cut in 2-inch sections	¼ cup rum
1 tbsp grated ginger	2 tbsp grated sweetened coconut
	· · · · ·

Heat butter in skillet over medium-high heat. When foamy, add bananas and ginger. Sauté for 2 to 3 minutes or until bananas are golden. Remove bananas to serving plates.

Add sugar and rum to skillet, quickly stirring into butter for 20 to 30 seconds or until sauce forms. Pour hot sauce over bananas and sprinkle with coconut.

RASPBERRY MOUSSE

SERVES 4

When my kids were little they used to call this raspberry gush. I would sometimes freeze it and serve it like ice cream. Garnish each serving with a few fresh raspberries.

3 cups fresh or frozen raspberries
¼ cup granulated sugar
1 cup whipping cream

Puree raspberries in food processor with sugar. Sieve to remove seeds.

Whip cream until stiff. Fold in raspberries. Serve in wine glasses.

RASPBERRY PARFAIT

In food processor or blender, combine 1 cup ricotta cheese, ¼ cup plain yogurt and 3 tbsp chopped fresh mint. Sweeten to taste and serve spooned over fresh raspberries.

SABAYON WITH PASSIONFRUIT

SERVES 2

A quick dessert spiced with ginger and topped with a luscious, fragrant fruit. Substitute raspberries, strawberries or blueberries if passionfruit is not available.

3 egg yolks

1 tbsp finely chopped preserved ginger in syrup

⅓ cup granulated sugar

⅓ cup white wine

2 tbsp passionfruit liqueur, optional

1 passionfruit, halved

• • • • •

Combine egg yolks, ginger and sugar in large heavy pot. Whisk on low heat until mixture doubles in volume and holds its shape.

Whisk in wine and liqueur. Continue to whisk until mixture is thick and creamy and has almost tripled in volume.

Divide sabayon between 2 wine glasses. Scoop out soft pulp from passionfruit and place on sabayon.

CHOCOLATE-DIPPED STRAWBERRIES

Wipe clean 1 pint fresh strawberries. Leave berries whole with stems attached. Melt 8 oz bittersweet chocolate in small pot on low heat. Using a fondue fork or skewer, dip strawberries into melted chocolate, making sure that at least half of each strawberry is coated.

Place strawberries on parchment paper to dry. Store in a cool, dry place. If you wish, inject liqueur into each strawberry after coating using a small kitchen syringe.

CARAMEL CREAM WITH FRUIT

SERVES 4

For caramel lovers what could be better than caramel-flavored whipped cream?

¼ cup granulated sugar	¼ cup sherry
1 cup whipping cream	¼ cup red currant jelly
1 tsp vanilla	1 lb mixed fresh berries or other fruit

Place sugar in small heavy pot on medium heat. Melt sugar, shaking pan occasionally. Cook until sugar turns a golden caramel color, about 4 minutes. Remove from heat immediately.

Add cream and vanilla to pot. (The mixture will bubble and spatter.) Stir together until well combined. Scrape into large bowl and chill.

Heat sherry and red currant jelly together until jelly dissolves. Toss with fruit. Chill until needed.

Whip caramel cream with electric mixer until it holds its shape.

Mound berries on serving dishes and top with caramel cream.

FIGS WITH RED WINE SYRUP

SERVES 4

An excellent dessert when fresh figs are available from late spring to fall. Mascarpone is a soft, high-fat Italian cream cheese with the velvety texture of super-rich whipped cream. If you can't find it, substitute soft cream cheese. For an extra-special presentation, garnish each serving with fragrant Kaffir lime leaves. These leaves of an Asian citrus fruit are available fresh or dried; use them sparingly in recipes.

4 oz mascarpone	Juice of 1 orange
4 tbsp granulated sugar	2 cloves
2 tbsp licorice or orange liqueur	pinch cinnamon
2 cups red wine	12 fresh figs

Beat together mascarpone, 1 tbsp sugar and liqueur.

Stir together red wine, remaining 3 tbsp sugar, orange juice, cloves and cinnamon in small pot. Bring to boil and boil until reduced to about 1/2 cup. Syrup should be slightly thickened.

Slice each fig into 3 pieces, down to but not through the root. Each fig should open up like a flower.

Place 3 figs on each plate. Fill centers with mascarpone and drizzle red wine syrup on plate.

SCOTCH CREAM

SERVES 4

An old-fashioned Scottish recipe for Scotch and marmalade lovers. For an attractive presentation, serve it in wine glasses and garnish with a piece of chocolate-coated orange rind.

1 cup whipping cream	1 tsp lemon juice
¼ cup Scotch	2 tbsp granulated sugar
⅓ cup marmalade	2 oz shortbread cookies, crushed

Whip cream until it holds soft peaks.

Stir Scotch, marmalade, lemon juice and sugar together in small bowl. Add marmalade mixture gradually to whipped cream, continuing to whip until cream stands in soft peaks. Do not overwhip.

Stir in shortbread crumbs. Refrigerate until ready to serve.

INSTANT CRÈME BRÛLÉE

SERVES 4

The secret to this recipe is to place the fruit and whipping cream in a very cold dish and refrigerate it before adding the caramel. This prevents the cream from melting when the hot caramel hits.

4 cups fresh fruit (seedless grapes, sliced bananas, peaches, mangoes, papaya, strawberries, raspberries)

2 tbsp liqueur of your choice

1 cup whipping cream

¾ cup granulated sugar

⅓ cup water

• • • • •

Place fruit in cold gratin dish. Add liqueur and toss. Return dish to refrigerator.

Whip cream until it holds stiff peaks. Spread on top of fruit, covering completely. Return to refrigerator.

Place sugar in small heavy pot on medium heat and add water. Melt sugar, stirring occasionally with clean wooden spoon. As soon as sugar has dissolved, raise heat to high and boil until mixture is a golden caramel color. Do not stir.

Pour thin stream of caramel immediately over whipped cream, covering surface. Hot caramel coming into contact with cold cream will bubble up and produce a marble effect. If any caramel remains, pour onto greased baking sheet, let harden and break up for garnish.

Return dessert to refrigerator as quickly as possible and chill for 30 minutes to 3 hours before serving.

WHITE CHOCOLATE PARFAIT

SERVES 8

A rich, creamy dessert that is sensational served with fruit or fruit sauces. Decorate it with dark chocolate shavings or leaves of dark chocolate.

10 oz white chocolate	6 egg whites
1 cup whipping cream	pinch salt
3 egg yolks	2 tbsp granulated sugar
2 tsp vanilla	• • • • •

Place chocolate in heavy pot over low heat. Stir occasionally until chocolate has melted and looks like thick cream. Remove from heat.

Heat whipping cream in separate pot until simmering.

Beat egg yolks with electric mixer, until thick and lemon colored. Whisk in warm whipping cream. Return mixture to pot and cook, stirring constantly, until mixture coats back of spoon. Remove from heat and beat in vanilla and melted chocolate until smooth. Cool completely.

Beat egg whites and salt with clean electric mixer until soft peaks form. Slowly beat in sugar until mixture is thick and glossy.

Stir one-quarter of whites into chocolate mixture, then fold in remaining whites. Pour into serving bowl and refrigerate until ready to serve.

MAPLE MOUSSE

SERVES 4

A low-fat version of a favorite dessert. Serve with dessert cookies (page 191).

½ cup maple syrup	2 egg whites
1 tsp grated lemon rind	2 tsp granulated sugar
2 cups drained yogurt	• • • • •

Heat maple syrup in pot, on medium heat, until ¼ cup remains.

Beat reduced syrup and lemon rind into yogurt.

Beat egg whites until frothy. Add sugar and continue to beat until egg whites hold soft peaks.

Fold egg whites into yogurt mixture. Spoon into glass dishes and serve.

DRAINED YOGURT

Line strainer with cheesecloth and place over a bowl. Add 4 cups plain yogurt to strainer and leave to drip, refrigerated, overnight. There will be about 2 cups yogurt remaining. Discard liquid. It should keep for about 3 weeks in the refrigerator. Use drained yogurt as a substitute for sour cream, or spread it on toast in place of butter.

FALLEN BROWNIE PUDDING

SERVES 4 TO 6

This gooey dessert is a chocoholic's dream, rather like a super-moist, extra-rich brownie. Serve it with ice cream or whipped cream flavored with grated orange rind.

½ cup butter	pinch salt
4 oz unsweetened chocolate	1 tsp vanilla
4 eggs, separated	½ cup all-purpose flour
2 cups granulated sugar	· · · · ·

Preheat oven to 350 F.

Melt butter and chocolate in heavy pot on low heat. Remove from heat and stir in egg yolks, sugar, salt and vanilla. Scrape into large bowl.

Beat egg whites in separate bowl until soft peaks form. Stir one-quarter of beaten egg whites into chocolate mixture, then fold in remaining egg whites. Gently fold in flour.

Pour batter into buttered 8-inch square baking dish. Place large pan of very hot water in oven. Place baking dish in larger pan. The water should come halfway up sides of baking dish.

Bake for 1 hour or until surface is crispy and inside is gooey and custardy.

Remove baking dish from larger pan to cool. Serve warm or cool with whipped cream.

THE WORLD'S EASIEST DESSERT COOKIE

MAKES ABOUT 60 COOKIES

These keep for weeks in an airtight container.

1 package wonton wrappers
Vegetable oil for frying
Icing sugar to taste
Cinnamon to taste

Separate wonton wrappers. Heat 1 inch oil in large deep skillet on medium-high heat. When very hot, add wrappers a few at a time and fry until golden, about 30 seconds. Remove with slotted spoon and drain on paper towels.

Combine sugar and cinnamon and sprinkle over cookies while still warm.

TUTTI FRUTTI

Combine your choice of fresh fruit and store-bought sorbet in this simple but spectacular dessert. Try to use contrasting colors of sorbet and fruit.

Toss fresh fruit with liqueur of your choice. Marinate until just before serving.

In wine glasses or Champagne flutes, alternate layers of sorbet and fruit, beginning and ending with sorbet. Top each serving with a sprig of fresh mint or rosemary and serve immediately with a storebought or homemade wafer cookie.

RASPBERRY THINS

MAKES 32 SQUARES

A moist chocolate square similar to a brownie but much richer. Cut small pieces. They freeze well and take about half an hour to reach room temperature.

4 oz unsweetened chocolate	1/2 tsp salt
1 cup butter	1 cup all-purpose flour
4 eggs, beaten	1 cup sieved raspberry jam,
1 tsp vanilla	apricot jam or marmalade
1 1/2 cups granulated sugar	Icing sugar

Preheat oven to 325 F.

Melt chocolate and butter in heavy pot over low heat. Remove pan from heat and stir in eggs and vanilla.

Combine sugar, salt and flour and stir into chocolate mixture. Scrape half of batter into buttered and floured 13 x 9-inch baking pan.

Freeze for 30 minutes or until layer is firm enough to spread thin layer of jam on top.

Spread jam and then remaining batter. Let stand for 15 minutes or until frozen layer has thawed.

Bake for 30 minutes or until a skewer inserted at the side comes out clean. (It will be slightly moist in middle.) Cool on rack. Sprinkle with sifted icing sugar before cutting into small squares.

SNOWDRIFTS

MAKES ABOUT 30 COOKIES

If the thought of combining chow mein noodles and white chocolate is a puzzlement to you, try this recipe; the sweetness of the chocolate is mellowed by the slight saltiness of the noodles. Substitute peanuts or other nuts for the cashews.

12 oz white chocolate

1 ½ cups cashews

2 cups chow mein noodles or pretzel sticks

Melt chocolate in large heavy pot on low heat, stirring frequently. Remove from heat and gently stir in cashews and chow mein noodles.

Drop by heaping tablespoon onto wax-paper-lined baking sheets to resemble little drifts of snow. Refrigerate until serving.

THUNDERCLOUDS

A crisp meringue-like chocolate cookie with a hint of ginger. Substitute chocolate wafer crumbs for ginger, if you prefer.

1 cup chopped bittersweet chocolate or chocolate chips	1 cup granulated sugar
3 egg whites	1/3 cup ginger cookie crumbs
pinch salt	1/2 tsp vanilla
	• • • • •

Preheat oven to 350 F.

Melt chocolate in heavy pot on low heat, stirring occasionally. Remove from heat and cool for 5 minutes.

Whisk egg whites and salt until stiff but not dry. Gradually beat in sugar until thick and glossy.

Fold in melted chocolate, ginger crumbs and vanilla. Drop by heaped teaspoon onto parchment-lined baking sheets.

Bake for 10 to 11 minutes or until crisp on outside. Cool for 2 minutes on baking sheet, then remove to wire rack.

CREAMY PLUM SQUARES

SERVES 6

This square is good served with a dollop of whipped cream or ice cream or as a snack with coffee. If you use prune plums, use about twelve but cut each one in half rather than quarters.

1 cup all-purpose flour	8 red or black plums, quartered and pitted
¼ tsp baking powder	½ cup granulated sugar
1 tbsp granulated sugar	½ tsp cinnamon
¼ tsp salt	1 egg yolk
½ cup butter	¼ cup whipping cream

Preheat oven to 350 F.

Sift together flour, baking powder, sugar and salt. Cut in butter until mixture resembles coarse crumbs. With fingers, pat into 9-inch square baking dish.

Arrange plums in rows over top of dough.

Combine sugar and cinnamon. Sprinkle over plums. Tap pan gently on counter to distribute sugar mixture.

Beat egg yolk and cream together. Drizzle over plums.

Bake for 40 to 45 minutes or until crust is golden and fruit is soft. Serve warm or cool.

RHUBARB CRISP

SERVES 4 TO 6

A family dessert for rhubarb lovers. The recipe was tested with hothouse rhubarb, which is sweeter than the outdoor green variety. Adjust the amount of sugar depending on the type you have.

2 lb rhubarb, trimmed and cut in 2-inch pieces	2 tbsp butter
1/2 cup brown sugar	• • • •
1 tsp dried ground ginger	**TOPPING**
1/2 tsp cinnamon	1/2 cup brown sugar
1/2 tsp grated nutmeg	1/2 cup all-purpose flour
2 tbsp grated orange rind	3/4 cup granola or rolled oats
	1/2 cup butter

Preheat oven to 375 F.

Mix together rhubarb, brown sugar, ginger, cinnamon, nutmeg, grated orange rind and butter in 11 x 7-inch baking dish.

Mix together brown sugar, flour and granola in separate bowl for topping. Cut in butter until mixture looks crumbly.

Sprinkle topping over rhubarb, making sure whole surface is covered.

Bake for 30 to 35 minutes or until top is browned and rhubarb has formed syrup.

PLUM CLAFOUTI

Clafouti is a type of fruit-filled pancake. It is often made with cherries, pears or peaches. It has a cakey, custardy texture and is wonderfully light after a heavy meal.

1 lb plums	½ cup all-purpose flour
¼ cup brandy or kirsch	pinch salt
2 tbsp butter	1¼ cups milk
3 eggs	2 tbsp icing sugar
⅔ cup granulated sugar	• • • • •

Preheat oven to 375 F.

Halve plums and remove pits. If plums are large, cut in quarters.

Pour brandy over plums and marinate for 30 minutes.

Lay plums in buttered baking dish large enough to hold them in one layer (press plums close together). Pour over any marinating liquid and dot with butter.

Whisk eggs and sugar until just combined. Sift in flour and salt. Whisk in milk. Pour mixture over plums.

Bake for about 40 minutes or until puffed and golden. Sprinkle with sifted icing sugar just before serving.

ORANGE CORNMEAL CAKE

SERVES 6

This very quick and flavorful cake is an Italian classic. The cornmeal adds a dense, crunchy texture. Serve with Oranges in Syrup or seasonal fruit and whipped cream.

1 cup cornmeal	1/2 tsp vanilla
3/4 cup all-purpose flour	1/2 cup butter, at room temperature
1 tsp baking powder	1 cup granulated sugar
pinch salt	• • • • •
2 eggs	ORANGE SYRUP
1 egg yolk	1/2 cup granulated sugar
1 tbsp orange juice	1/2 cup water
2 tsp grated orange rind	1/4 cup orange juice

Preheat oven to 350 F.

Combine cornmeal, flour, baking powder and salt.

Stir together eggs, egg yolk, orange juice, orange rind and vanilla in separate bowl.

Cream together butter and sugar with electric mixer in large bowl until light and fluffy.

Beat in egg mixture, then flour mixture. Continue to beat until batter is pale yellow, about 3 minutes.

Pour batter into buttered and floured 8-inch square cake pan and bake for 40 minutes or until toothpick inserted into cake comes out clean.

Make syrup while cake is baking. Combine sugar and water in small pot. Slowly heat until sugar dissolves, then bring to boil. Boil for 5 to 6 minutes or until mixture forms a syrup. Remove from heat and cool for 2 minutes. Add orange juice.

Cool cake in pan on wire rack for 10 minutes. Turn out onto plate. Poke holes in cake with toothpick, then brush with syrup. As syrup is absorbed, brush with more syrup.

ORANGES IN SYRUP

Remove peel and white pith from 4 oranges. Slice oranges into thin rounds.

Make a syrup by boiling together 1/2 cup granulated sugar and 1/2 cup water for 5 minutes. Remove from heat and flavor with 1 tbsp orange liqueur or orange juice concentrate. Pour syrup over oranges.

RUM AND RAISIN SAUCE

MAKES ABOUT 1 1/2 CUPS

Serve hot with vanilla ice cream. The sauce reheats perfectly.

1/2 cup corn syrup	1/2 tsp vanilla
1/2 cup brown sugar	1/4 cup dark rum
1/4 cup cream	1/4 cup raisins
2 tbsp butter	. . . . .

Combine corn syrup, brown sugar, cream and butter in heavy pot. Bring to boil and boil for 5 minutes.

Add vanilla, rum and raisins and simmer for 1 minute.

KAHLUA SAUCE

A chocolaty rich sauce that can be served warm over ice cream or poached pears.

4 oz semisweet chocolate	¹/₂ cup whipping cream
¹/₂ cup water	¹/₄ cup Kahlua
¹/₂ cup granulated sugar	· · · · ·

Melt chocolate over low heat in small heavy pot. Stir in water and sugar. Bring to boil and simmer for 5 minutes.

Add cream and Kahlua and simmer for 5 more minutes or until sauce coats back of spoon.

CHOCOLATE

I like to use good-quality European chocolate in cooking. *Unsweetened chocolate* contains no sugar and is used in recipes where a dense, bitter chocolate taste is needed. It is often combined with bittersweet chocolate for the most intense flavor.

Bittersweet chocolate has some sugar added and has a concentrated chocolate flavor. *Semi-sweet chocolate* contains even more sugar, although it can be used interchangeably with bittersweet.

Milk chocolate contains milk solids; do not use it in cooking unless a recipe specifically calls for it.

White chocolate is a mixture of sugar, cocoa butter, milk solids and vanilla. Don't use white chocolate that contains vegetable shortening—the taste will be bland and dull.

Index

K

Kahlua sauce, 200
Kidney beans, *See also* White beans
    chili, 103
        vegetarian, 142
    refried, 141

L

Lamb:
    chops, 114
    grilled Bombay-style, 118
    rack of,
        with arugula and vinaigrette, 115
        cooking, 115
        with mustard mint topping, 116
    roast, honey-glazed, 117
Lasagne:
    topless, 130
    vegetable, 129
Latkes, 161
Leeks:
    pasta with, 123
    and squash gratin, 153
Lemon:
    chicken with, 83
    grilled slices, 83
Lentil(s):
    braised, 140
    soup, 23
Lettuce:
    salad with pears and roquefort, 164
    Tuscan salad, 169
Lime:
    sauce, 85
    spiced chicken, 82

M

Maple:
    cream, 21
    -glazed pork chops, 110
    mousse, 189
Mascarpone, figs with red wine syrup, 185
Mayonnaise:
    coriander chili, 50
    tarragon, 52

Mediterranean-style:
    phyllo cigars, 13
    salmon, 57
    tart, 42
    tuna salad, 52
    vegetable lasagne, 129
Mexican-style:
    chicken soup, 16
    rice casserole, 104
Mirin, about, 68
Miso:
    about, 26
    ginger vinaigrette, 164
    soup with spinach and noodles, 26
Mole sauce, 80
Moroccan-style:
    chicken tagine with green olives, 89
    chickpea and onion couscous, 137
    quick couscous, 137
Mouclade, 75
Mousse, raspberry, 182
Mushroom(s):
    caviar, 6
    on country bread, 45
    fried rice, 136
    pasta with sausage and, 122
    and potato gratin, 156
    rice, 134
    risotto, 132
    sandwiches, 37
    sauce, 101
    stock, 37
    and watercress stir-fry, 152
Mussels:
    cleaning, 76
    mouclade, 75
    wok-steamed, 76

N

Niçoise salad, 53
Noodles, *See also* Pasta; Rice noodles
    miso soup with spinach and, 26
    scallops with, 74
    seared tuna with, 68
    with spicy peanut sauce, 128